Metric Dashboards for Operations and Supply Chain Excellence

Metric Dashboards for Operations and Supply Chain Excellence

Jaideep Motwani and Rob Ptacek

business**expert**
Press

Metric Dashboards for Operations and Supply Chain Excellence
Copyright © Business Expert Press, LLC, 2014.

First published in 2014 by
Business Expert Press, LLC
222 East 46th Street, New York, NY 10017
www.businessexpertpress.com

ISBN-13: 978-1-60649-768-5 (paperback)
ISBN-13: 978-1-60649-769-2 (e-book)

Business Expert Press Supply and Operations Management Collection

Collection ISSN: 2156-8189 (print)
Collection ISSN: 2156-8200 (electronic)

Cover and interior design by Exeter Premedia Services Private Ltd., Chennai, India

First edition: 2014

10 9 8 7 6 5 4 3 2 1

Printed in the United States of America.

Abstract

Over the last decade Lean and Six Sigma methods and tools have helped organizations improve to historic productivity levels with the data driven, systematic elimination of waste, and improvement of flow. Today many organizations have enjoyed the benefits of Lean and Six Sigma initiatives, and are looking more to sustain the gains, and aggressively drive a systematic and ongoing approach to improvement and problem solving. The concept of diminishing returns applies here in the early stages when organizations were able to find "low-hanging fruit" and to quickly make significant improvements. Now the easy work is done, and organizations need a simple yet systematic approach to continuing their continuous improvement efforts.

The term scoreboards and dashboards are quite common, and many organizations have them. However, the author's observations are that there are many problems common to most organization dashboards. Specifically, we find that organization dashboards do not provide the following key attributes:

Key Attributes for Scorecards and Dashboards

1. Clear and understandable to the worker or performer—More often than not we find metric dashboards contain the language of leadership, and not the worker. As a consequence, the worker does not understand or care about the metric, and the metric has no value in driving improvements in performance
2. Contain the vital few performance indicators—Rather we find an information overload of too many metrics at all levels of organization. We again find worker apathy, and metrics that do not drive improvement and problem solving, and behavioral issues are a result.
3. Clearly connected to the next level and the organization strategy—Typically we find a huge disconnect between organization strategy and key metrics measured. Workers that do achieve their goals see no positive consequence, and worker attitude suffers.

4. Action and improvement focused—Many organization dashboards are not linked in any way to current improvement or corrective action projects. Yes dashboards exist, but they are more of a show piece on the wall than a systematic way to improve the organization. The charts and graphs simply become wallpaper.

Operations and supply chain leaders will benefit from this book by developing a clear understanding of why and how metric scorecards and dashboards can be used as a powerful data driven improvement tool. The authors demonstrate in this book how key components of visual management, scorecards, and dashboards drive leader standard work and improved overall performance of work teams. The authors demonstrate how the proper use of these simple tools can drive organizations continuing efforts to identify and reduce waste, improve performance, and speed delivery.

This book illustrates visual management, scorecards, and dashboards for a full range of organizations, and focuses on operations and supply chain management areas. By covering these tools in these environments in a story book format, organization leaders can begin to understand how these methods and tools can be applied in their organizations. Through a unique and captivating story of a frustrated operations leader, discovering the power of these tools, the authors present a compelling argument to begin using metric scorecards and dashboards. This story illustrates the discovery, application, and transformation of an operations and production supply chain.

Keywords

metrics, scorecards/dashboard, key performance indicator (KPI), waste elimination, continuous improvement, balanced scorecard/dashboard, lean, Lean Sigma

Contents

CHAPTER 1

The Organizational Measurement Challenge: What's the Score? Are We Winning?

Just as the whistle blew to start the second half, there was a loud "POP," and the lights went out in the gymnasium. It was the season finale of the championship basketball game between the Supply Chain Hoopsters and the D-Line Production teams. The groans of the faithful crowd of coworkers could be heard through the pitch-black darkness. As the generator kicked in, the lights began to flicker an eerie orange glow. The game would go on.

"The game can go on when the scoreboard starts working," said Jim, the official scorekeeper.

"What do you mean?" said Larry, the Supply Chain Hoopsters team captain.

"I think the 'pop' we heard was the scoreboard shorting out. I'll see if we can get another one," Jim said, as he ran off to the equipment room.

After several anxious minutes, the crowd began to rumble. Jim returned empty-handed.

"We'll just have to go without a scoreboard," Jim proclaimed.

"How will we keep score?" said Joe, the D-Line Production team captain.

Jim said, "Well, I have the official scorebook, I'll just keep it there, and see how things go."

After several more minutes of discussion, the team captains and other officials agreed to give it a try.

The plan was to keep the score in the score book at the scorer's table, the time on Jim's wristwatch, and for Jim to periodically update everyone on the status. The first half ended with the Supply Chain Hoopsters team leading the D-Line Production team by 5 points. Several players had committed fouls, and Jim provided a detailed report to each team before the start of the second half.

"Okay, this is as good as it's going to get," said Stripes, the lead referee. "Let's get this game going!"

Stripes blew the whistle and handed the ball to the inbounding player to get the second half started.

Things went along fairly well for the third period, and much of the fourth or last period. About half way through the last period, during a time-out, one of the team members asked Joe, "What's the score? Are we winning?" Joe said, "I'm not exactly sure, but just keep up the hard work."

Sandra, a fan, came into the game late, and asked her friend, "What's the score? Are we winning?" Her friend said she wasn't exactly sure, but the team was playing hard.

As the game drew near the end, the need for information became more and more critical. The excitement level in the crowd was at a fever

Imagine for a moment the scenario: you are watching or playing your favorite sporting event, and there is no scoreboard or clock. How will the fans know the status of the competition or the time left? How would the players know what to do? In our basketball game, should they shoot three-point shots or try to stall? Should they intentionally foul or avoid contact? In American football, should the team try to stay inbounds or go out of bounds? Kick a field goal or try for a touchdown. In soccer should your team stall with an extra defender, or pull people up for a more aggressive offensive attack. Pull the goalie, or use more defenders? In golf, do you need a miracle shot, or can you play it safe? Lag putt or drive it past the cup?

How enjoyable would the situation be for the fans or the players, or even the referee, whose calls may determine the outcome of the game? In any competitive event, the players, coaches, fans, and referees need to know the score and game status instantly and continuously, in real time, to do their best.

pitch! This was the championship after all. Information such as the score, time left, fouls, and time-outs had to be known practically every instant. Jim did his best to shout out relevant data as he kept the score, but the crowd, the referee, and most of the team players really didn't know exactly what the situation was.

Back at the championship game, the Supply Chain team had just stolen the ball and was in the middle of a 3-on-2 fast break when Jim stood up at the scorer's table and waved his arms above his head as though he was doing jumping jacks, and shouted, "Games over!"

Stripes, the referee, blew the whistle and ran over to the scorer's table. The crowd was softly muttering, wondering what was going on. Both teams were walking about, and also wondering what was going on. After a minute or two, Stripes raised his voice to the teams and the fans, and proclaimed, "The D-Line Production team wins by one point!"

The D-Line team screamed with joy, and began a celebration at center court. Half the fans cheered and applauded, and the other half moaned in shock, disbelief, and utter confusion.

"This is not right. This game is under protest!" cried Larry the Supply Chain team captain. "This is ridiculous! We thought we were ahead. We would have played differently had we known the score and time left. This can't possibly be fair! This is ridiculous!"

Ridiculous as it may sound, many organizations run their businesses like this. Their leaders, workers, and their families are "in the dark" regarding the critical information regarding how the organization is doing day-to-day. They literally do not know if they are winning or not. Joe wondered, "Wouldn't it be nice if every organization developed a customized dashboard that was visually appealing and communicated high-level summary information of how the organization was performing? This would help employees to find out and understand early tends, patterns, and correlations in data."

Larry added, "Our organization already has a system in place. However, to prevent this ridiculous situation from repeating, we need to design a back-up system that would keep the score accurately if we lose power in the future."

Joe agreed, and Larry left upset and frustrated with what had just happened.

The Janesville Area Corporate Basketball
Year-End League Results

The Janesville area corporate basketball league consisted of two divisions of five teams each. The league standings and results are as follows:

Janesville Area Basketball League Year End Standings

East Division Teams	W–L	Winning Percentage
Supply Chain Inc	17–2	89.5
A-1 Construction	14–5	73.7
Comfort Eats	9–9	50.0
Bob's Bakery	5–14	26.3
First Bank of Janesville	2–17	10.5

West Division Teams	W–L	Winning Percentage
D-Line Production	16–3	84.2
Janesville Medical Center	12–7	63.1
Jeb's Job Shop	9–9	50.0
Janesville Power Company	7–12	36.8
Janesville Intermediate School District	3–16	18.7

League Championship Game Results

D-Line Production   League Champion
Supply Chain   Second Place

Discussion Questions

1. Why is it critical to keep a scoreboard? Does your organization have a scorecard to keep track of the key metrics/indicators on a consistent basis?
2. What do you think of Larry's comments "This is not right. The game is under protest!" What would you have done in this situation?
3. What lessons can we all learn from this situation? What can we do to prevent encountering a similar situation at our workplace?

CHAPTER 2

Measuring Operations and Supply Chain Performance: Winners Work

The day after the championship game was like any other day for the D-Line Production team captain Joe. Joe was also a team leader in the shop at D-Line Products. D-Line Products was a high-volume manufacturer of component parts. Since they run large machines that require massive time to change over from one job to the next, they run large batches of parts. They store these parts in their inventory racks, and use them when their customer releases orders.

A typical day for Joe was spent matching up schedules to actual production output, setting direction for his team members, getting information on what job to run next, and solving problems that seemed to come up on a regular basis. Basically, Joe was the "answer man" for the production team. He kept quite busy throughout the day.

This day happened to be the day of the monthly highlights meeting, where the leaders of the company reported on the company's performance. Everyone always looked forward to this meeting as that is where they would hear if they would receive bonus for the month or not.

This, combined with winning the corporate basketball league championship, had everyone in a good mood. As Joe went from work station to work station the congratulations were flowing.

"Nice job last night Joe," said Bill from production line one. "Are we going to get a big bonus today?" He continued.

As Joe made his rounds, and collected his daily data from each cell, he couldn't help thinking about how strange it was at the game last night without a scoreboard, and how upset Larry from Supply Chain Inc. was about the loss. He wondered if the protest would really happen.

Joe collected the data as he did every day, and made it back to his office to do the calculations. Joe had to load the data into the computer, and update several spreadsheets, and then he could print the reports on how they were doing. Once he got the reports printed, Joe would then make the rounds again providing the new reports to everyone, and make or adjust plans to catch up or reassign people to other areas if they were ahead.

Joe kept thinking about how slow this process was, and that the extra time talking about the game had really put him behind. He thought he'd never get it all done before the plant-wide performance meeting, so he tried to keep a quick pace.

By the time of the plant-wide performance meeting, Joe had still not made it to two of the production teams. He made a mental note to himself to get with them right after the meeting.

The meeting began with the owner saying that she had some good news and some bad news. Everyone's heart sank. She went on to describe a situation where the company was doing well, but not well enough for a bonus. As happy as they were about the basketball championship, they were even more disappointed to hear this news. They were on an emotional roller coaster. They thought they were doing so well but the charts and graphs of the month-end meeting told a different story.

Sales were up, which was the good news, but almost every other indicator was going the wrong direction. Why did it take until the month end to figure this out? Joe's reports during the month kept things going, but didn't really provide the information that prepared the workers for this!

After the meeting everyone was looking for Joe.

"Why didn't you tell us this Joe?" said one cell operator.

"If we knew, we could have done something about it," said another.

"Well," Joe said, "I kept telling everyone the information I had as quickly as I could get it!"

Finally, Joe got to the areas he had missed before the meeting. The workers there asked Joe, "How are we doing today? Are we doing good enough to get a bonus next month?"

Joe had to confess that he wasn't quite sure, but if they kept working hard they should be able to get a bonus next month.

"How are we doing now?" the next team asked.

"Just keep working hard," Joe explained.

Another team leader was heard to say, "This is not right. We deserve a bonus! We've been working hard. This is ridiculous! We thought we were doing well! We would have done something differently had we known about the bonus. This can't possibly be fair! This is ridiculous!"

Joe thought again about the basketball game. His work situation seemed strangely familiar. The Supply Chain Inc. players were playing hard and thought they were winning the game. His workers were working hard, and thought they were winning a bonus. For different reasons, neither the players nor the workers really knew the score, or they might have done things differently in effort to win. This bothered Joe and the workforce for some time.

Discussion Questions

1. Discuss the process used by Joe in collecting data for preparing the report for the plant-wide performance meeting? What would you have done differently?

2. What do you think of the owner's comments at the start of the meeting? What can the owner do to make sure the employees understand and interpret the charts and graphs properly prior to the meeting in order to avoid any surprises?

3. Do you think the team leader was justifiable in making the comment that they deserved the bonus? Shouldn't a team leader know better?

CHAPTER 3

Organizational Measurement Methods and Tools: Training Day

After a somewhat frustrating week at work, Joe made a promise to himself to make improvements before the next month performance meeting, but he wasn't quite sure what to do. To make things worse, he had a training class his boss had signed him up for, which would take him out of the office for a couple days. The training session was going to begin this week, and Joe thought to himself that he'd better try to get ahead of things before he had to go to the training sessions.

It was the first day of the training class, and Joe was not looking forward to the class this morning. Things at work had gotten quite busy, and he could barely keep up himself. With Joe gone today for the training session, Bill would have to take over his daily duties of data collecting and reporting. Nonetheless, Joe was committed to the training. It was on continuous improvement, something he knew he needed.

The class was being held at the Comfort Eats out by the highway. So Joe grabbed his coffee, and got an early start as this was a long drive for him. Once at the class, he saw that many local organizations were represented. He hoped he'd see Larry, the Supply Chain Inc. basketball team captain. He had not seen him since the championship game, and he wondered if he was still upset.

As the training session started, the facilitator asked everyone to introduce his or her company. Some organizations had several people at the session, but everyone elected a spokesperson to introduce his or her company. Joe went first.

D-Line Products

D-Line Products is the largest employer in the area, employing around 300 people. D-Line Products is a high-volume manufacturer of component parts. We run large machines that required massive time to change over from one job to the next, so we try to run large batches of parts. We store these parts in inventory racks, and then use them when our customers release orders. We are organized into several departments or work-teams.

Larry from Supply Chain Inc. was there, and he went next. Joe made the following notes from the introductions.

Supply Chain Inc.

Supply Chain Inc. is a professional service organization specializing in supply chain management and improvement. Several local companies use Supply Chain Inc. for materials and supplies sourcing, training, and managing their supplier and logistics performance. Supply Chain Inc. is a small firm employing 25 people.

A-1 Construction

A-1 Construction is a general contractor of mid- to large-scale building projects. They have a fluctuating workforce, depending on active projects. They have 15 full-time employees, but manage several subcontractors. Their expertise is in contractor selection and project management. A-1 Construction wins many local contracts in the Janesville area. They own some heavy equipment, but mostly use other subcontractors to accomplish the work.

Comfort Eats

Comfort Eats is a hotel, restaurant, and bar at the highway interchange. In this service-oriented business they have a very well-known name. People come from great distances to dine in their five-star upscale dining room. They have recently hired a new chef who is making even more improvements. They have about 60 employees.

Bob's Bakery

Bob's Bakery is a large-scale bakery. They weigh up ingredients, mix, mold, bake, and package bread for the tri-county area. They have 95 full-time employees on three shifts. Trucks are moving production in and out of their facility 24 hours a day.

First Bank of Janesville

The First Bank of Janesville consists of four branch banks servicing the local Janesville area. They provide basic banking services, savings and checking accounts, home, car, and business loans, as well as other financial services. They have a total of 35 employees, mostly tellers.

Janesville Medical Center

Janesville Medical Center is the main hospital in the Janesville tri-county area. They provide a full range of healthcare services. Their workforce consists of doctors, nurses, administrators, and many other healthcare professionals. They are one of the larger employers in the area employing over 200 people.

Jeb's Job Shop

Jeb's Job Shop does just about anything from fixing cars to fabricating custom metal production. They are a true job shop in that they produce many different items, in very small quantities. They are the classic low-volume, high-product mix organization. They spend a great amount of time tracking and following orders through the shop. They only employ around 15 people total, and many of them are long-term highly skilled employees. They work only one shift.

Janesville Power Company

The Janesville Power Company is a continuous processing organization. They run a coal-burning plant that must stay running around the clock, or the lights will go out in the town. Their workforce consists of operators, service and repair people, as well as administration and office personnel. They have about 130 employees running three shifts, seven days a week.

Janesville Intermediate School District

The Janesville Intermediate School District is the main K-12 school system in the area. They are responsible for developing and delivering high-quality curriculum to the young men and women in the Janesville area. They too are a large employer, employing over 165 teachers, counselors, coaches, administrators, and the like.

The training session was on visual management and corporate dashboards. Something Joe had read about in his continuous improvement book. The morning went fairly smoothly. The lecture was good, and thought-provoking. Joe learned that visual management techniques are used to help people understand their environment at the speed of sight, to ensure that the right things get done right, right on time. A quote was provided in the class that goes like this:

> Create a work environment that is self-explaining, self-regulating, and self-improving—where what is supposed to happen does happen, on-time, every time, day or night.
>
> Gwendolyn Galsworth

As part of the training session, the facilitator assigned participants to teams. Each team was responsible for listing the needs and benefits for visual management. Based on their research and discussions, the group agreed on the following five reasons:

1. Visual management is a technique employed whereby control of an activity or process is made clearer, easier, and more effective by deliberate use of visual indicators, signals, controls, and guarantees.
2. Visual management techniques capitalize on the age-old adage that "a picture is worth a thousand words." If done properly, visual management techniques speed up analysis, understanding, alignment, and reaction time to key issues.
3. Visual management techniques can take on many different forms. Visual management techniques help workers and leaders operate more effectively to achieve goals and objectives.
4. Visual (or audio) management techniques will effectively communicate the information needed for decision making. Visual management techniques are one part of an overall communication system of an

organization to ensure standards are met and work is completed on time, and can continue to the next process without errors.

5. Visual management techniques should be used (or at least considered) at every juncture of an improvement project. Visual management techniques are used to identify conditions that may cause an error, or if an error occurs, what must be done to prevent it from becoming a defect.

[*Source: Visual Systems* (AMA, 1997) ISBN: 0-8144-0320-4.]

After agreeing on the need for visual management, the facilitator went on to describe the four levels of visual controls:

Level 1—Indicators: provides information about the immediate environment, area, department or process. These are passive and people may or may not notice them or respond to them. It is the lowest form to influence behavior. Examples of Level 1 visual controls are as follows:
- "Allergy Alert" is highlighted in red on the patient's chart and ID bracelet.
- Signs, posters, maps, arrows, and so on.
- Color-coding emails or other electronic files and folders
- Floor lines
- Work instruction books
- Color-coding emails or other electronic files and folders

Level 2—Signals: provides a visual or auditory alarm that should grab your attention and is a warning that a mistake or error is about to occur. Signals have a higher level of influencing behavior. People still may ignore these, but they are very aware that something may be wrong. Examples of Level 2 visual controls are as follows:
- Andon lights
- Audible "beep" when bar code scans properly
- An automatic horn on a fork lift when backing up
- Performance dashboards on desktop screens
- Green light in front of cashier indicating that the register is open for next customer
- A sound (or chirp) from the copy machine indicating service is required or ink is low

Level 3—Controls: physically or electronically limits or causes behavior to be modified to prevent the wrong thing from happening in a process. These are more aggressive than Levels 1 and 2, and are used to guide and control behaviors so that only the correct option is selected. Examples of Level 3 visual controls are as follows:
- Double palm buttons that must be pressed to engage or cycle a machine
- Machine safety guarding
- Locks, security codes, and so on
- Email rules and filters
- Dropdown menu selections

Level 4—Guarantees: ensures that a correct decision is made. They are the highest level of visual control (most likely referred to as mistake proofing devices). Visual guarantees force the correct decisions to be made and are mistake proofing controls and devices (next section). Examples of Level 4 visual controls are as follows:
- Guide pins that only allow a tool to be placed in the proper direction
- Sensors that stop equipment if parameters are not met
- Swipe cards for secure entry or time keeping
- Box sizes that only allow the proper quantity to be packed
- Usernames and passwords to an account

A discussion among the participants occurred regarding where their organizations were currently and where they would like to be.

Joe asked the facilitator, "When creating and employing visual management tools improvement teams need to decide which level is most appropriate for the situation."

The facilitator replied, "Clearly, Levels 3 and 4 are the most comprehensive in terms of ensuring that an error or mistake does not occur, but the solution may not always be possible or cost-effective. Consider information requirements and availability both upstream and downstream of the area being addressed. Once the information to share has been determined, visual controls can be selected or created and implemented. Implement visual controls in a PDCA fashion to ensure success."

The participants all agreed and shook their heads. The facilitator then decided to move along and asked the participants if they were familiar with the term corporate (or team) scorecard.

The representative from Janesville Medical Center raised his hand and said, "Corporate (or team) scorecards and dashboards are a type of visual management technique used to clearly illustrate status and progress to goals of the organization or group." Another participant from Bob's Bakery added, "Scorecards are typically used to document the key performance data, and dashboards are where the data is summarized and displayed for easy analysis and alignment." The facilitator agreed with both their statements and added that "Scorecards can also display the key data, but sometimes do not show clearly enough longer term trends. He then showed examples of scorecards and dashboards (see the following).

Scorecard Examples

Standard
300pc/HR

TIME	PCs	Total
8 AM	250	250
9	300	550
10	310	860
11	200	1060

Dashboard Examples

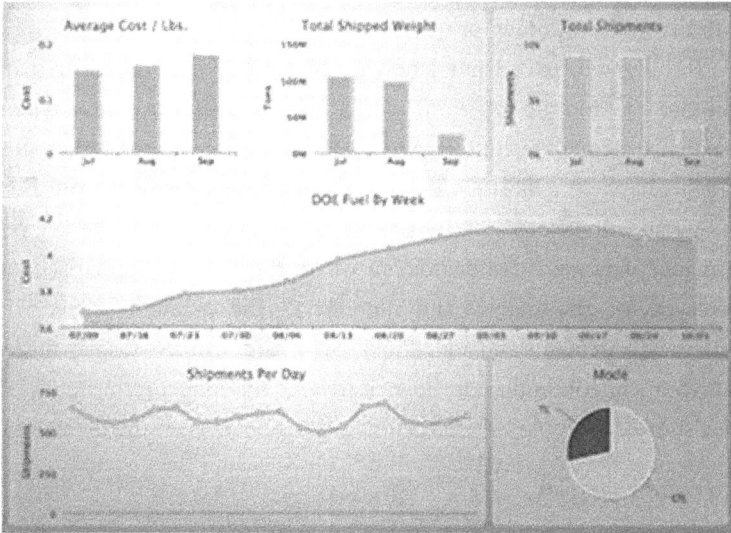

Source: M33 Integrated Solutions. 511 Rhett St., Greenville, SC 29601 (864) 672-2862.

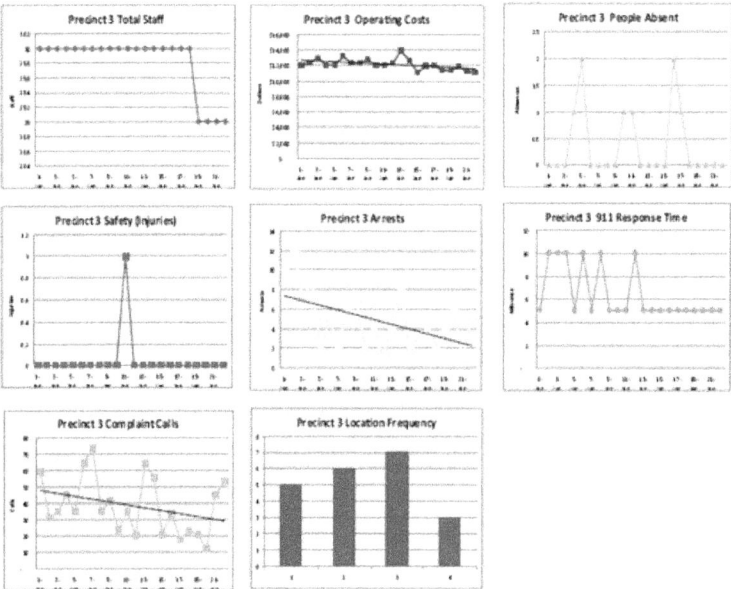

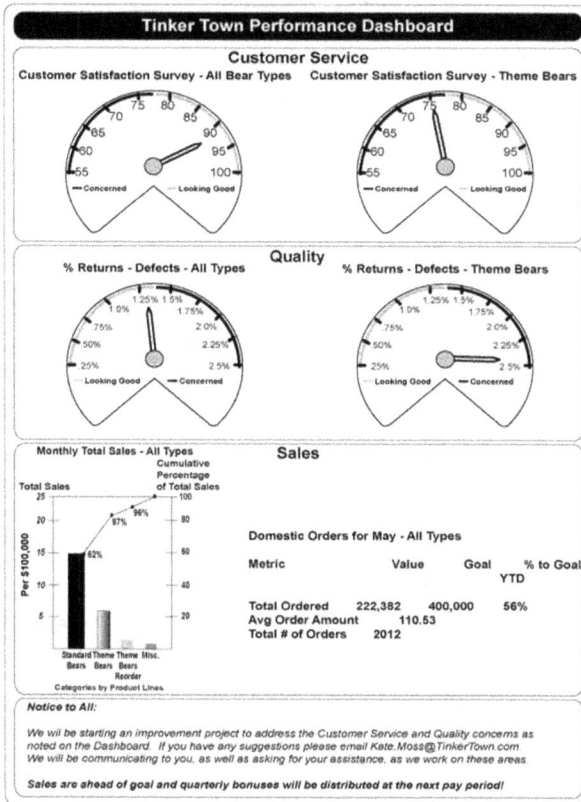

Tinker Town Performance Dashboard

Customer Service

Customer Satisfaction Survey - All Bear Types   Customer Satisfaction Survey - Theme Bears

Quality

% Returns - Defects - All Types   % Returns - Defects - Theme Bears

Sales

Monthly Total Sales - All Types

Cumulative Percentage of Total Sales

Total Sales

Per $100,000

Categories by Product Lines

Domestic Orders for May - All Types

Metric	Value	Goal	% to Goal YTD
Total Ordered	222,382	400,000	56%
Avg Order Amount	110.53		
Total # of Orders	2012		

Notice to All:

We will be starting an improvement project to address the Customer Service and Quality concerns as noted on the Dashboard. If you have any suggestions please email Kate.Moss@TinkerTown.com We will be communicating to you, as well as asking for your assistance, as we work on these areas.

Sales are ahead of goal and quarterly bonuses will be distributed at the next pay period!

By late morning, Joe's stomach was growling with hunger. He couldn't wait for lunch. During lunch, Joe thought he'd have time to drive back to D-Line Products for a quick check in. As soon as the facilitator dismissed the group for lunch, Joe was out of the door and into his car. He first stopped at the local drive-through Burger Sling, and placed an order. Joe noticed that they had a picture menu for their drive-through window. All he had to do was look at the picture menu and say the number into the microphone. "How easy was that?" he thought.

Discovery

Joe was making good progress until he got to the train tracks. As he approached the tracks, he noticed the flashing lights, and the gates beginning to swing down to close. As he stopped and put the car in park, he noticed more visual indicators on the dashboard of his car. All kinds of symbols that provided a clear and instant indication of what each knob, gage, or button were for. He thought about how difficult it would be to drive a car without any visual indicators or signals on the dashboard. "How would anyone know what the buttons, knobs and indicators meant? I guess after a while people would figure things out," he thought.

The train was a long one. Joe had finished his burger, and the train continued to rumble by. He thought he'd better turn around and get back to class. He only hoped that Bill was taking care of things at work. As Joe swung the car around and made his way back to the Comfort Eats, he made note of the many road signs and lines and lights that indicated what to do, and what not to do. Maybe this visual management and dashboard training had some merit, but Joe still wasn't convinced.

The afternoon session of the class was uneventful. Joe's mind drifted in and out of the training session as he was concerned about how Bill was doing at work. He wondered if he'd have time to stop by before he had to pick his father up for his bowling league that night.

As the facilitator began to wrap things up for the day, Joe was watching the clock. Just as he thought they were finished, Joe heard the dreaded word, "homework." The facilitator challenged the group to observe 7–10 visual management, scorecard, dashboard items, or all outside the classroom, in non work-related areas. Joe thought, "Great, just what I need, homework!"

Time was short now, and Joe had to run right to his father's house to pick him up for the bowling league. Joe had promised his father he'd be there tonight to take him to the lanes, and watch the team. Joe made it to his father's house, and after some small talk, made his way to the bowling alley.

As Joe sat at the team table and watched the teams bowl, he couldn't get over the speed and accuracy of the computer scoring system. After each ball was rolled, the score would be automatically posted on the large screens above the alleys. The running grand total of the number of pins, and the number of pins each team was ahead or behind was updated after each roll!

Joe chuckled to himself as he thought how advanced the bowling alley was compared to D-Line Production.

The Next Day Homework

The next day at work Joe had a mess on his hands. Bill had done a good job at gathering and reporting the data, but new orders had come in, and the work teams were getting behind. After his morning rounds, Joe had to spend most of the rest of the day rearranging the work schedules, attending meetings, and trying to catch up on all the e-mails he'd missed while he was at training.

Near the end of the day Joe looked at his planner and saw that he had the second half of the visual management and dashboard training course tomorrow! He had a sinking feeling as he'd not even started on his homework assignment yet. "Now where did I put my notes on the homework?" he thought as he rifled through his cluttered notebook. "Ah-ha!" he said, as he pulled a ruffled paper out of the mess.

"OBSERVE VISUAL MANAGEMENT ITEMS IN NON-WORK-RELATED AREAS," he read. "This should be easy," he thought. "I remember seeing a few items the day of the class when I went to lunch." Joe quickly started the following list:

Visual Things

1. Flashing red lights at the train tracks
2. Barrier gate at the train tracks

3. The dashboard in my car
   a. PRND12 gear shift indicator
   b. Speedometer
   c. Fuel gauge
   d. Radio settings, and so forth
4. Traffic lights, signs, signals, lines, and arrows
5. Parking lot lines
6. Billboards

   The pace of Joe's writing slowed. "What about at the bowling alley?" he thought, and continued his list.

7. Bowling scoreboards

"What else do we keep score of?" Joe thought. A smile came to Joe's face and he quickly added "basketball scores" to his list. With that thought Joe happily crammed the list into his folder and headed home.

Enlightenment

The next day at class the facilitator led a discussion on the homework assignment. Joe's list was good, and his classmates came up with even more items. Joe was starting to realize just how "visual" his world really is.

For a class exercise, they broke out into small groups, and were asked to identify "Things we measure in our personal life." The brainstorming went quickly. Joe was the scribe for his group, and he could barely keep up. He wrote the following on the white board:

Things We Measure in Our Personal Life

1. Weight
2. Blood pressure and sugar
3. Cholesterol
4. Heart rate
5. Temperature
6. Checkbook balance
7. Bowling scores
8. Basketball scores and statistics by player
9. Golf score
10. Miles run

11. Time riding
12. Antler points and Boone and Crockett score
13. Words per minute
14. Intelligence quotient (IQ)
15. Gas gage
16. Speed
17. Things we cannot afford to run out of run out, such as gas, milk, toilet tissue, and so forth.
18. Anything competitive. In any competitive event or situation, a score is kept in some way. It's the very nature and definition of competition.

Businesses are in an extremely competitive environment every day!

The class discussed why we measure things. Their conclusions were that "We measure what's important to us. If it's important, odds are you measure or keep track of it!"

The next assignment was for each organization to identify the things that are important to them, and their key measures at work. What measures are currently in place at their company? What is their competitive score? The facilitator directed the groups to put the key measures into the categories of: customer focus, quality, delivery, productivity, people, and financial. This activity consumed much of the morning session. Joe had practically forgotten about poor Bill making the rounds for him at work.

After lunch each organization shared their key measures. It was interesting to see that there were many similarities, as well as key differences. Joe took the following notes from each organization's presentation:

Supply Chain Inc.

- Customer focus: Sales revenue, new accounts, new proposals
- Quality focus: Customer evaluations
- Delivery focus: Commitments met on time
- Productivity focus: Revenue per person
- People focus: Turnover
- Financial focus: Profit, return on investment (ROI)

A-1 Construction

- Customer focus: Sales revenue, new projects, bids
- Quality focus: Customer satisfaction sign-offs, customer complaints, budget to actual performance
- Delivery focus: On-time projects
- Productivity focus: Revenue per person, projects per person, materials use to budget
- People focus: Turnover, safety
- Financial focus: Profit, ROI

Comfort Eats

- Customer focus: Sales revenue, room fill rates, new menu items, and specials
- Quality focus: Customer surveys at tables, customer complaint and feedback, tips, reject and wrong order rate
- Delivery focus: Drink and food delivery times
- Productivity focus: Sales per person, table turnover rates
- People focus: Turnover, attendance, training, and advancements
- Financial focus: Profit, ROI

Bob's Bakery

- Customer focus: Sales revenue, new product offerings, new customers
- Quality focus: Scrap or rejects per day
- Delivery focus: On-time deliver to customers
- Productivity focus: Sales per person, units per person, materials use to budget, improvement savings per person
- People focus: Turnover, attendance, loss time injury rates, training
- Financial focus: Profit, ROI, performance to budget

First Bank of Janesville

- Customer focus: New accounts, new production
- Quality focus: Customer surveys and feedback, error rate of transactions, balancing records

- Delivery focus: Average customer wait times
- Productivity focus: Transactions per day per person
- People focus: Focus-group discussions, turnover, training
- Financial focus: Profit, ROI

Janesville Medical Center

- Customer focus: Revenue, new offerings or services provided
- Quality focus: Error rate per person and team, customer complaints, exit surveys
- Delivery focus: Speed of service transactions, average customer wait time
- Productivity focus: Sales revenue per employee, patients per month per person, improvement savings per person
- People focus: Turnover, safety, training
- Financial focus: Profit, ROI

Jeb's Job Shop

- Customer focus: Sales revenue, new accounts, quotes
- Quality focus: Scrap and reject rates, rework costs, quote accuracy
- Delivery focus: On-time delivery to the customer commitments
- Productivity focus: Sale per person, contribution margin per person
- People focus: Turnover rate, attendance, safety, training, improvement ideas submitted per person
- Financial focus: Profit, ROI

Janesville Power Company

- Customer focus: Sales revenue, new clients or hook-ups, outages
- Quality focus: Outages per month not weather related, customer surveys and feedback

- Delivery focus: Average time to restore power after outage, days on-line at full capacity
- Productivity focus: Sales per person, kilowatt hours supplied per person
- People focus: Employee surveys, turnover, safety, training
- Financial focus: Profit, ROI, performance budget

Janesville Intermediate School District

- Customer focus: Revenue, class offerings, teacher- or counselor-to-student ratio
- Quality focus: Graduation rates, standardized test scores
- Delivery focus: Percent students graduating on time, days open to schedule
- Productivity focus: Student-to-teacher ratio, student-to-administration ratio
- People focus: Turnover, training, employee surveys
- Financial focus: Profit, ROI, performance to budget

Finally, Joe presented his key measures.

D-Line Production

- Customer focus: Sale revenue, new customers, new jobs, customer satisfaction calls or surveys
- Quality focus: Daily scrap and reject rates, rework, defective parts per million (DPPM) rates
- Delivery focus: On time in full deliveries to schedule, schedule attainment, per day, week, month, and year
- Productivity focus: Contribution margin per person, sales per person, labor cost as a percent of sales
- People focus: Turnover, attendance, training, employee morale surveys
- Financial focus: Profit, ROI

Performance Measurement Summary Table. Key Performance Indicator Matrix

Key Performance Indicator Category	Supply Chain	A-1 Construction	Comfort Eats	Bob's Bakery	First Bank of Janesville	Janesville Medical Center	Jeb's Job Shop	Janesville Power Company	Janesville Intermediate School District	D-Line Production
Customer focus										
Sale revenue	X	X	X	X		X	X	X	X	X
New accounts, projects, or items	X	X	X	X	X	X	X	X	X	X
New proposals, quotes, or bids	X	X		X	X		X			X
Fill rates or ratios			X			X		X	X	
Quality focus										
Customer satisfaction evaluations, surveys, or feedback	X	X	X		X	X				X
Customer complaints		X	X	X	X	X		X		X
Tips			X							
Rejects, reworks, or wrong orders and Scrap		X	X	X	X	X	X			X
Success rates									X	
Test scores									X	
Delivery focus										
On-time delivery or commitment to the customer	X	X		X			X		X	X
Delivery lead-time	X		X		X	X	X	X		X
Schedule attainment	X					X		X	X	X
Productivity focus										
Revenue per person	X	X	X	X		X	X	X		X

(Continued)

Performance Measurement Summary Table. Key Performance Indicator Matrix **(Continued)**

Key Performance Indicator Category	Supply Chain	A-1 Construction	Comfort Eats	Bob's Bakery	First Bank of Janesville	Janesville Medical Center	Jeb's Job Shop	Janesville Power Company	Janesville Intermediate School District	D-Line Production
Projects or units per person		X		X	X	X		X	X	X
Materials used to budget	X	X		X						X
Table turnover rates			X							
Improvements per person						X				X
Contribution margin per person								X		X
People focus										
Safety or accidents		X		X		X	X	X		X
Loss time accidents				X						X
Turnover rates	X	X	X		X	X	X	X	X	X
Attendance		X	X	X			X			X
Training and advancements		X	X	X	X	X	X	X	X	X
Surveys or focus-group discussions and feedback								X	X	X
Financial focus										
Profit (EBITA)	X	X	X	X	X	X	X	X	X	X
Return on investment (ROI)	X	X	X	X	X	X	X	X	X	X
Performance to budget	X	X	X	X	X	X	X	X	X	X

The facilitator then concluded the session by saying, "Many of the measurements that determine the health of a business are common regardless of the organization or type of business. Likewise, some measures for the health of an individual are common, such as blood pressure, blood sugar, cholesterol, and the like. Most of these measures for businesses are reviewed on a monthly basis. While this is good, it seems at times to be too late to do anything about it. It was like driving a car by looking in the rear-view mirror, or getting a detailed report on your average speed for a trip, but not having a speedometer to monitor during the trip. The monthly numbers do not drive problem solving and improvement behaviors quickly enough."

Joe was looking for something more real time that could drive action, problem solving, and improvement, like sporting event scoreboard.

Discussion Questions

1. Briefly discuss the term visual management techniques. How does your organization use visual management techniques?
2. Discuss the four levels of visual control? What level of visual control does your organization use? What would you recommend they use?
3. What level of visual control would you recommend Joe's organization to use and why? How should they go about implementing one?
4. Summarize the different visual systems that Joe encounters or discovers in this chapter. What can Joe learn from them?
5. What do you think of the concluding statement the class made? "We measure what's important to us. If it's important, odds are you measure or keep track of it!" Does your organization practice the above statement?
6. What are some of the key performance measures you track in your organization? How do they match up with the ones highlighted in the Key Performance Indicator Matrix? Are there some key indicators that have not been listed? What can your organization learn from this table?

CHAPTER 4

Developing Organizational Measures: The Plan

The next day Joe saw Larry from Supply Chain Inc. at the Burger Sling.

"Hey Larry, how are you doing? You're not still mad about the game are you?" Joe said smiling as he reached out to shake Larry's hand.

Larry grabbed Joe's hand firmly and shook it vigorously, and said, "Mad? I was never mad, just frustrated. That power outage was ridiculous. We should have never agreed to play under those conditions, but what's done is done. I just wish the officials would run the league as well as I'm expected to run Supply Chain."

"What does that mean?" asked Joe.

"Well, for starters our scoreboard works!" said Larry, and both men laughed.

Larry continued, "We help our clients source materials and supplies at the total lowest delivered cost. We track and monitor the total system performance at critical checkpoints, and then react and respond to prevent errors and wastes from occurring."

"Do you use scorecards and dashboards?" asked Joe.

"Absolutely!" replied Larry emphatically. "In fact our entire operation is driven by our corporate dashboard and our daily scoreboard. Our call-center service team has huge scorecards and dashboards on an 8-foot-by-12-foot screens in front of them all day long. They do not go home until we win. You should come over and look at our office someday. We might be able to help you as well. We've been trying to get D-Line Products as a customer for some time now, and since you cheated us out of the basketball championship, I think you owe it to me to come over and visit. We track and order status on an hourly basis, as well as supplier performance metrics on a weekly basis. We also have tracking systems and dashboards for sales forecasts, inventory or warehousing, reverse logistics, and sustainability. For sustainability we use the triple bottom-line metric categories of financial, environmental, and social, but it works out about the same."

Joe interrupted, "What are you doing right after lunch? I can come over right now for a look, if that works for you."

"I can, let's take a minute to eat, and then go right to my office," replied Larry.

Over lunch, Joe and Larry talked about the training session they recently attended, and of course, the basketball game.

Once at Larry's office, Joe was amazed. It looked more like a command center or an air traffic control area rather than a Supply Chain Inc. office. On the walls there were huge screens visible to everyone. The screens indicated in real time how the work was going. Items like number of loads scheduled and their status were clearly shown on the large screens. Loads at risk were highlighted so that everyone could see who was working on it, and the pending issues.

Source: M33 Integrated Solutions, 511 Rhett St, Greenville, SC 29601 (864) 672-2862.

Larry talked Joe through the processes and showed Joe how they at Supply Chain Inc. used scorecards and dashboards. Joe was impressed and already thinking of his next steps at D-Line Products.

Joe thanked Larry for the brief tour, and headed back to work. Before Joe left, Larry asked Joe to tell Anne, D-Line's Supply Chain Manager, to set up a meeting so he could show her the benefits of outsourcing some of the logistics and supply-chain management activities to Supply Chain Inc. Joe promised he would set up the meeting with Anne, and made a quick exit.

Joe's plan was to ask his team members and supervisors what was important to them and their teams at work. What measures would tell people throughout the day how they were doing, and if they were winning. Joe began by making his own notes on what he monitors in the categories of customer, quality, delivery, productivity, people, and financial.

Joe's Daily Work Scorecard measures are similar to the monthly company measures, but more specific, more real-time indicators. They are as follows:

- People focus: attendance and accidents.
- Delivery focus: on-time in full (OTIF) deliveries to schedule, schedule attainment, less than lead time (LTLT) orders taken and achieved.
- Quality focus: daily scrap and reject rates, and rework.
- Productivity focus: actual pieces or units produced per person per day versus scheduled pieces or units produced per day per person. Stock outs, Labor cost as a percent of sales.
- Customer focus: customer returns and complaints.
- Financial focus: sales dollars shipped daily and bonus achievement.

Joe's next step was to review this list with his supervisors and team leaders, and get their buy in. His first attempt at a daily scorecard is as follows.

Joe's Daily Scorecard

Area	Measure	Who Tracks the Data	3-Aug	4-Aug	5-Aug	6-Aug	7-Aug
People	Attendance percent	Rich					
	Consecutive days safe	Rich					
Delivery	Daily on-time in full deliveries to schedule (OTIF)	Joe					
	Daily schedule attainment	Joe					
	Less than lead time (LTLT) orders achieved as a percent of total LTLT orders taken	Bill					
Quality	Scrap pieces	Pat					
	Rejected units	Bill					
	Reworked items	Denny					
Productivity	Actual units per person per day versus scheduled units per person per day	Rich					
	Stock outs	All					
	Labor cost percent of sales	Rich					
Customer	Customer return dollars	Denny					
	Customer complaints	Rich					
Financial	Bonus status	Joe					
	Sales dollars shipped	Joe					

At the meeting with the team leaders most of the team leaders and supervisors agreed with the key measures Joe had defined. Many of the measures were the same measures that Joe collected each day. Bill mentioned that for some of the measures, once a day is still too late, and that he thought they should measure some of the items every hour, or at least two or three times throughout the day. They agreed to develop some simple tracking sheets to collect and display these data at the appropriate locations. Joe made a commitment to collect data and post the daily scorecard at each work cell each day as he made his daily rounds. Some of the data entry, such as consecutive days safe, they assigned to their team members to log in daily.

After some concern from John regarding how this would be more work, Rob mentioned that it's just like keeping score in golf as we did this weekend in the two-person best ball, and Rob tossed the card over the meeting table. The leaders laughed and continued to work. "I guess if it's important, we can do It," said John.

With general agreement, the team made assignments. The next step was to try it out for a couple weeks in a Plan-Do-Check-Act improvement spirit. So the plan was set, for the next two weeks everyone would keep track of the key measures that occurred and record them on the scorecard in their work areas, Joe would collect the numbers daily, and update and post the consolidated production department scorecard in each work area everyday. At the end of the two-week trial period, Joe would schedule another meeting to evaluate how the system worked, and determine if they want to make any improvements.

"Have a great weekend everyone, see you Monday!" said Joe as he closed the meeting.

Discussion Questions

1. What do you think of Larry's comment that his entire organization is driven by corporate and daily dashboards? What can your organization

learn from Larry's description of how they use dashboards and score-cards? What did Joe observe and learn from his visit to Larry's office?

2. How would you describe Supply chain Inc.'s visual system? Do you think it is necessary for all organizations to monitor critical performance measures on a real-time basis?

3. Do you think it is a good idea for Joe to ask his team members and supervisors of what was important to them and their team at work? Is transparency, communication, and employee involvement critical to developing a successful performance measurement system?

4. Critically evaluate the process and the Daily Scoreboard developed by Joe. Do you think that the next step agreed on by the team was the right approach to use?

CHAPTER 5

Key Enablers—Policy Deployment, Accountability Sessions, Employee Training and Involvement, and Improvement Tool Selection and Application

As Joe completed the scorecards he started thinking about some of the things Larry had told him about the keys to making this work. Larry had clearly indicated that there were four enablers that drove success with the scorecards and dashboards. Joe called his team to educate them on what he had learned from Larry.

Organizational Enablers

Joe kicked off the meeting by stating that there are four organizational enablers for scorecard and dashboard success that should be in place prior to initiating scorecards and dashboard management techniques.

Bill immediately asked, "I am clueless. What do you mean by the term 'organizational enablers?'"

Joe responded, "The enablers allow an organization to engage, and will affect everything done during the implementation. Each enabler will involve understanding, educating, and involving our people. The enablers provide the foundation on which all will rest. The proper balance of the four enablers also becomes critical during the transformation. We must work to understand and adjust the balance between four enablers.

The four organizational enablers (4 Ps) are as follows:

Enabler 1: Principled Leadership: Management Commitment and
   Leadership
Enabler 2: People Focus: Training and Engagement
Enabler 3: Policy Deployment: Goal Alignment–Ownership–Account-
   ability
Enabler 4: Practical Application: Using the right tool for the job."

After hearing Joe's explanation, the entire team nodded their heads. Bill
again raised his hand and asked Joe, "Can we learn more about each of
the enablers and what we need to do?"

Joe smiled and said, "Yes, that's why we are here. He then went on to
explain Enabler 1.

Enabler 1: Principled Leadership: Management Commitment and Leadership

Scorecards and dashboards must be driven from the top down. Top management must make a 100% commitment to positive change and must
be 100% convinced that a consistent and disciplined approach to scorecards and dashboards represents the best opportunity for continued or
newfound success. A partnership led by top management, and developed
and implemented by a motivated workforce, will ensure scorecards and
dashboards are not only implemented, but sustained."

After listening to Joe's passionate explanation, Rob asked, "Do you
mean that leaders and managers must 'Walk the Talk?'"

Joe said, "Exactly. The phrase 'Walk the Talk' means that a leader or
manager's behavior must match his or her expressed strategy for the organization. A leader or manager must be willing to do and sacrifice at the
same level that they expect from others. People quickly see where leaders
do not walk the talk, and this can lead to confusion, and lack of trust in
an organization, which foils most improvement efforts.

It is vital to recognize that scorecards and dashboards will not work
without total commitment from management. A CEO reading about
scorecards and dashboards in the *Wall Street Journal* on a flight coming

home from vacation, and then telling his top manager that 'it sounds like a good idea' does not reflect or constitute a long-term desire to implement and engage.

Management commitment must be driven by a passion to improve. The top manager must be totally involved in the implementation of any improvement effort. Even, if that first improvement project involves only three people, top level commitment must be present."

Bill intervened and asked Joe, "How do we know if our management is committed?"

Joe responded, "We know management is committed when they are:

- Committing the necessary resources to the improvement initiatives
- Being present at the first meetings
- Providing coaching and counseling to the team when needed
- Displaying interest in the team's progress by attending meetings
- Rewarding and recognizing the team's effort
- Having empathy when the team is struggling

That is not an exhaustive list, but it does show a general framework for how management commitment can be manifested."

Rob nodded his head and agreed with Joe. He immediately added that when he had undertaken a course in Lean Sigma Service transformation, the facilitator had clearly stated that, "Leaders must consistently identify, define and communicate the need to improve, the vision of what to improve to, and provide leadership and resources to make the improvements."

Joe got very excited and screamed, "Yes, you are absolutely right. To define and communicate the need to improve, leaders often use a Mission Statement, which can include, the mission, vision, and values."

Bill, the inquisitor, asked, "What do you mean by mission, vision, and values?"

Joe responded, "Mission statement is a basic statement of the identity of an organization and the purpose or mission. Organization leaders often see this as the bland, generic mission statement on a conference room wall. To a savvy leader, the mission and mandate statements provide the opportunity to define the organization and the customers or markets they serve. Savvy leaders use the mandate to define the compelling need to change and achieve excellence. Leaders use the mandate to identify the organizations stakeholders and priorities. The mandate if done properly can be a rallying point for the members of the organization. It is a key to establishing a self-motivating environment, which leads to a continuous process improvement, customer, and team-focused culture.

Many organizational leaders speak of developing 'culture.' The mandate is foundation document to do this. Do not skip the mandate and mission if you are serious about pursuing excellence. The best-run organizations develop the mandate in a participative manner in an effort to develop a high level of commitment and understanding at all levels. Supply Chain Inc.'s mission is as follows.

Mission Statement:
Supply Chain Inc. will meet or exceed customer requirements, regarding quality, cost and delivery, while continually improving our commitment to customer satisfaction."

Bill nodded his head and said, "That makes a lot of sense. However, how is the vision different from the mission?"

Joe responded, "The vision defines the future identity of the organization. Visions are sometimes relegated to the conference room walls as well, and this is a missed opportunity for the leader. Vision statements can help to control the behaviors of the organization. They define what the organization is trying to become. The vision can define the guidelines for behavior change and improvement.

Leaders need to initiate the vision, and then develop a shared understanding and support. This is best done through a participative development process. The vision should be sufficiently detailed and comprehensive to allow the members of the organization to 'see the picture' of what they are striving to become. Too vague of a vision tends to confuse people, and does not provide enough detail to modify behavior. Too detailed a vision tends to confine an organization to over-burdensome bureaucratic behaviors.

A simple way to define a vision for an organization is to define the current state of behaviors. What are currently acceptable behaviors for the organizations' members?

- Is it acceptable to not clean up after yourself?
- Is it acceptable to show up late for meetings?
- Is it acceptable not to follow work standards?
- Are people treated fairly and equitably for their contributions?
- Is it acceptable to pass poor quality?
- Is it acceptable to scream and shout at people?
- Does the organization learn from their failures?
- There is little accountability or discipline to rules and goals.
- Do all levels receive proper training?

Then, define the new vision by defining what the organization wants to become.

- Always clean up after yourself. Leave an area cleaner than when you arrived.
- Be on time for all meetings. Start all meetings on time.
- Work standards and rules are followed by all.
- People are treated equitably. There is no favoritism.
- Do not pass on poor quality.
- Treat people with respect and dignity. Value and train on diversity.
- Develop a system to learn from failures.
- A systematic approach for accountability and discipline exits at all levels.
- A training and education plan exits for all members of the organization.

Developing a vision is the responsibility of management. It is not always easy, but well worth the effort if done properly. The vision provides the framework for holding people accountable, and improving the organizational culture."

He then concluded by saying that the Supply Chain Inc.'s vision is as follows.

Vision Statement:

Supply Chain Inc. will be known as the outstanding supplier and employer of choice for Supply Chain and Logistics optimization and management. We will achieve our goals safely and with total customer satisfaction and operational excellence as our focus. We will be known for our customer service, quality, and engaging work environment. *"Nobody does it better!"*

The team decided to take a short break before they discussed the other three enablers. As soon as the break was over, Joe went about explaining the second enabler.

Enabler 2: People Focus: Training and Engagement

He started by saying, "This enabler helps employees understand why current ways of doing business may not be good enough. As companies grow and take on more work, waste reduction must become prevalent in all aspects of the organization. Employees must recognize that every type of task has a cost associated to it. This segment will explain how to effectively communicate this need for change, and create a learning and action-oriented organization.

The introduction and initial implementation of any improvement effort must change behavior first if a continuous improvement culture is to emerge. Change cannot be accomplished overnight. Employees must understand that positive change will contribute to the organizations and their personal long-term success."

Bill interrupted, "Joe, doesn't this mean that understanding human behaviors and attitudes within an organization are critical to achieving success in any improvement initiative; especially in a service organization where employees frequently interact with the customer."

"Yes," said Joe with a big smile on his face. "The overall improvement models are simple. It requires a diligent and focused effort from both managers and employees. Established work habits are difficult to break. Training, education, discipline, dedication, and determination are required to move an organization forward. Small successes will create the momentum to move from the simple behavior and attitude change to a continuous organizational culture.

The key to any improvement effort is the continual, daily effort to improve. As behavior changes, you will want to initiate a reward and recognition system to acknowledge the changes that are occurring. Quick adapters to change will embrace this system. They will see the benefits immediately. Slow adapters may fight the system and hold on to old habits. Slow adapters will struggle for a while; however, be patient as the system will speak for itself when implementation is under way and employees start to experience the benefits. Engage people on improvement teams, and expect them to be accountable and take responsibility for improvements. It is their job after all.

Reducing waste and costs and improving the total customer satisfaction will lead to overall business growth and profitability. Growth and profitability are essential for any business to survive. Through implementing a Lean Sigma transformation, a business will survive, become stronger, and will be able to provide wage and earnings growth, and advancement in a safer, more stable work environment."

Everyone nodded their heads as if to inform Joe that they had fully understood what he had just said. They were now ready to learn about Enable 3.

Enabler 3: Policy Deployment: Goal Alignment–Ownership–Accountability

Joe started by saying that "this enabler is a basic form of performance management. It involves setting goals, assigning responsibility, and providing follow-up to ensure appropriate progress is being made. Specific and measureable goals, with deadlines, must be established and communicated to all members of the organization. The goals must be aligned with the organizations strategy, and assigned to individuals and teams. As simple as it sounds, many organizations do a poor job with this key enabler."

Rob immediately raised his hands and said, "Joe, did you just say that goals must be aligned to an organization's strategy in order for the strategy to be realized? If so, how should we go about doing it?"

Joe responded, "Yes, I did say that. Goals must also be aligned between all areas and departments within an organization. Goal conflict or misalignment within an organization erodes teamwork and impedes progress. The process of policy deployment puts action to the strategic plan, and aligns goals, measures and actions." He then went about asking his team if they had heard the acronym SMART.

No one in his team had heard about this acronym. Joe then explained, "How the acronym SMART helps leaders and managers establish goals. The acronym SMART stands for the following.

S = Specific
M = Measurable
A = Assigned
R = Realistic
T = Time-bounded

People do not mind being held accountable to SMART goals. Goals meeting the SMART criteria at all levels lead to an environment where people can motivate themselves to high levels of performance and achievement. Organizations that do not bother with SMART goal setting are plagued by confusion, conflict, and chronic underachievement."

The team then discussed that it is the leader's responsibility to create a work environment where people and organizations can be inspired to achieve their full potential. Setting SMART goals, providing resources, and holding people accountable to achieve the goals is part of creating such an environment. Scorecard and dashboard-driven environments are exciting and engaging for people at every level of an organization. Everyone knows how their role, and how they help the organization succeed. If a leader wants to improve organizational culture SMART goal setting and fair accountability is a solid place to start.

A consistent and predictable accountability system should also be employed. Too often people get frustrated with leadership when the rewards and consequences do not match the measures. Have you ever been disciplined for following procedures? Many leaders do not understand the unintended consequences of their actions.

They agreed that a series of supportive work sessions be established for daily, weekly, and monthly dashboard monitoring. The basic agendas for such work sessions should be as follows:

Standard Scorecard/Dashboard Work Session Agenda

1. *What happened since our last session as compared to what was supposed to happen?*
2. *What is the scorecard or dashboard indicating?*
3. *What corrective or preventative action items should we take up and who should do them by when?*
4. *What has to happen or should we anticipate between now and our next work session?*

After agreeing on the Agenda, Joe moved to discussing the last enabler.

Enabler 4: Practical Improvement Tool Application

Joe started his explanation by saying that "not every improvement tool will apply to every organization and situation. It is critical for an organization to recognize this and to select the appropriate methods and tools that will help their organization eliminate wastes. While some improvement tools are universal such as value mapping, 5S or visual management, other improvement tools may simply not apply to a specific environment. For example, the concept of pitch or queue time may be more appropriate than Takt time for a particular service process."

Joe then said that he strongly believed that improvement tool selection and application are more important than trying to use every tool on the internet. He warned his team not to get caught up in a "program of the month" syndrome. He reiterated that the objective of scorecards, dashboards, and other improvement tools is to eliminate waste, not to just use tools.

Rob asked Joe if he could give an example. Joe immediately responded, "just as an auto mechanic will diagnose or define a problem, then pull the appropriate tool from their tools box; diagnostic tools such as scorecards and dashboards are used to see the waste in a common way, before appropriate improvement or problem-solving tool can be applied. Let the process needs determine tool to use. He cautioned his tea, that they should not randomly apply as many improvement tools as possible but to use a focused, systematic approach to continuous improvement."

Joe was glad he documented all of this, and surprised he could remember it. The next step was to get the scorecards in place and work the plan.

Discussion Questions

1. Critically discuss the four organizational enablers for scorecard and dashboard success. Were or are these enablers present and/or aligned in your organization?

2. Do you agree with the following statement "Scorecard and dashboards must be driven from the top down?" Is this true in your organization?

3. What are your thoughts about the three leadership responsibilities in a Lean Sigma Service transformation? What can your management team learn from these responsibilities?

4. Is your organization people focused? What can your organization do to become more people focused?

5. Does your organization do a good job in policy deployment? What could they do differently?

6. Do you agree with the statement that "not every improvement tool will apply to every organization and situation"? What universal and other improvement tools does your organization focus on?

CHAPTER 6

Using Scorecards and Dashboards: Working the Plan

The week went well, and the data were flowing. By Wednesday evening, the scorecard looked like this:

Area	Measure	Who Tracks the Data	3-Aug	4-Aug	5-Aug	6-Aug	7-Aug
People	Attendance percent	Rich	100%	100%	100%		
	Consecutive days safe	Rich	123	124	125		
Delivery	Daily on-time in full deliveries to schedule (OTIF)	Joe	100%	98%	100%		
	Daily schedule attainment	Joe	91%	95%	82%		
	Less than lead time (LTLT) orders achieved as a percent of total LTLT orders taken	Bill	100%	100%	100%		
Quality	Scrap pieces	Pat	12	35	26		
	Rejected units per day	Denny	0	2	1		
	Reworked items	Denny	0	1	0		
Productivity	Actual units per person per day versus scheduled units per person per day	Rich	110%	106%	101%		
	Stock outs	All	0	0	1		
	Labor cost percent of sales	Rich	14.70%	20.80%	16.60%		

(Continued)

Area	Measure	Who Tracks the Data	3-Aug	4-Aug	5-Aug	6-Aug	7-Aug
Customer	Customer return dollars	Denny	$122	$0	$0		
	Customer complaints	Rich	1	0	0		
Financial	Bonus status	Joe	Yes	Yes	Yes		
	Sales dollars shipped	Joe	$34K	$25K	$30K		

Bill caught up with Joe on Thursday morning, and said, "Joe we've been talking a bit, the numbers are all good, but there is no feeling for if we are doing well or not, you know, are we meeting the goals? Even on the golf course we have 'Par' for the hole, something to shoot for." Joe said, "You're right! We talked about this in my recent class and with Larry. I'll put some goals on the scorecard, and use some visual indicators to show if we're doing good or bad."

After Joe met with some of the company leaders, he put the goals or targets on the scorecard and used some visual indicators to show status. At the work areas, some of the leaders began to use "smiling faces" on their area scorecards to show if they met the goals or not.

The updated scorecard with goals and with "green" meaning goal met, and "red" meaning goal not met visual indicators is shown as follows:

Area	Measure	Goals	3-Aug	4-Aug	5-Aug	6-Aug	7-Aug
People	Attendance percent	100%	100%	100%	100%		
	Consecutive days safe	Increase	123	124	125		
Delivery	Daily on-time in full deliveries to schedule (OTIF)	100%	100%	98%	100%		
	Daily schedule attainment	100%	91%	95%	82%		
	Less than lead time (LTLT) orders achieved as a percent of total LTLT orders taken	100%	100%	100%	100%		

Area	Measure	Goals	3-Aug	4-Aug	5-Aug	6-Aug	7-Aug
Quality	Scrap pieces	<15	12	35	26		
	Rejected units per day	0	0	2	1		
	Reworked items	0	0	1	0		
Productivity	Actual units per person per day versus scheduled units per person per day	≥100%	110%	106%	101%		
	Stock outs	0	0	0	1		
	Labor cost percent of sales	>15%	14.70%	20.80%	16.60%		
Customer	Customer return dollars	$0	$122	$0	$0		
	Customer complaints	0	1	0	0		
Financial	Bonus status	Yes	Yes	Yes	Yes		

Note: ■ Red   ▨ Green

The teams found that this was helpful to keep them up to speed on how they were doing as a production department, but the real-time charts they were keeping at their workstations gave them better information that they could make adjustments to throughout the day to make sure they met the goal. This was actually the intent, to provide information that would allow teams to adjust to meet the goals. This was truly like a scorecard for them, and they were working! The team members began to look at the scorecards regularly in their "daily huddle" work sessions, and strive to achieve the goals throughout the day.

The production teams also found that there were some indicators that they could not directly control on a real-time basis. Measures such as the sales per day, customer complaints per day, and attendance were difficult for the teams to affect throughout the day. They felt they were appropriate to track for informational purposes, but what really drove the teams should be the productivity, quality, and delivery measures.

At the follow-up work session, the leadership team reviewed the following data:

	Measure	Goals	3-Aug	4-Aug	5-Aug	6-Aug	7-Aug	8-Aug	9-Aug	10-Aug	11-Aug	12-Aug
People	Attendance Percent	100%	100%	100%	100%	99%	100%	100%	100%	100%	99%	100%
	Consecutive Days Safe	Increase	123	124	125	126	127	128	129	130	131	132
Delivery	Daily on-time in full deliveries to schedule (OTIF)	100%	100%	98%	100%	100%	97%	96%	99%	98%	100%	99%
	Daily schedule attainment	100%	91%	95%	82%	100%	95%	92%	100%	99%	99%	100%
	Less Than Lead time (LTLT) orders achieved as a percent of total LTLT orders taken.	100%	100%	100%	100%	100%	100%	100%	99%	100%	100%	100%
Quality	Scrap pieces	<15	12	35	26	18	12	22	34	13	12	9
	Rejected units per day	0	0	2	1	0	0	0	0	0	1	0
	Reworked items	0	0	1	0	2	0	3	24	6	4	8
Productivity	Actual units per person per day versus scheduled units per person per day	≥100%	110%	106%	101%	100%	106%	110%	120%	116%	118%	110%
	Stock outs	0	0	0	1	0	0	0	0	1	0	0
	Labor cost percent of sales	<15%	14.70%	20.80%	16.60%	15%	12%	16%	11%	12%	10%	9%
Customer	Customer return dollars	$0	$122	$0	$0	$0	$90	$0	$0	$0	$0	$0
	Customer complaints	0	1	0	0	0	0	0	1	0	0	0
Financial	Bonus status	Yes	Yes	Yes	Yes	Yes	Yes	Yes	Yes	Yes	Yes	Yes
	Sales dollars shipped	≥ $30K	$34K	$25K	$30K	$38K	$42K	$28K	$22K	$36K	$45K	$43K

Note: ▉ Red   ▉ Green

Clearly, the team had opportunities for improvement. The team felt that the scrap and rework problems caused them to miss the production schedule, which lead to the late delivery issues, and although things seemed to be getting better, they should do something more to improve. Overall, the scorecard seemed to be working well; the teams were talking about the critical topics each day, and asking good questions, but they were not sure what to do next. Joe told the team to continue to keep up on the scorecard, and to do what they could to improve quality and he would call Larry to ask some questions about what to do next.

Discussion Questions

1. Critically discuss the process and updated scorecard developed by Joe's organization. What can other organizations learn from this?
2. Do you agree with the production team that some indicators could not be monitored on a real-time basis? Have they identified the right indicators that they cannot monitor on a real-time basis?
3. Have the teams identified the right opportunities for improvement? Can you think of some other improvements that the team can make?

CHAPTER 7

Case Review: Metrics in Action!

Joe scheduled another visit with Larry. When Joe arrived, Larry invited him into a conference room and asked, "What's up Joe? Why the need for another session? Do you want a rematch of the basketball championship game?"

"No, nothing like that, we won that game fair and square," replied Joe. "I want to pick your brain on scorecards and dashboards again."

"Pick away," replied Larry.

"Well since we last spoke, we've implemented hour-by-hour scorecards at the work centers, and are rolling the real-time work center data up onto daily area scorecards. We're seeing some indicators that are doing well, and some that are not. We even think we see a correlation between our scrap and rework rates and our delivery performance, but we're not quite sure what to do next," explained Joe. "I want to understand your process better so I can lead our improvement," he added.

Larry waived his hand and said, "Let's take a walk Joe. As we go I'll explain and show you the impact of our systematic approach to our work. You see it all starts with standard work for leaders."

Joe interrupted, "For leaders?"

"Yes, for leaders." continued Larry. "You see every person in our organization, from the CEO to the first-level supervisor, every leader, and every person has standard work."

"What standard work looks like for a leader?" asked Joe.

Larry stopped by a wall chart (shown in the following) and described each level of leader's standard work.

	Daily	Weekly	Monthly	Semi-Annually	Annually
Corporate leader	1. Follow appropriate work instructions and procedures, and complete Job Description activities	1. Daily activities plus the following	1. Weekly activities plus the following	1. Review all organizational level KPIs, goals, and individual subordinate performance. Check for alignment with organization strategy. Modify as needed	1. Review all organizational level KPIs, goals, and individual subordinate performance. Check for alignment with organization strategy. Modify as needed
	2. Complete and analyze required productivity reports, including hour reports and job reporting—corporate-level data.	2. Establish rolling weekly agenda and conduct weekly meeting with each plant manager—use the DMAIC, after action review (AAR), and project management format. Meeting should focus on KPIs, CIs, and countermeasures	2. Complete and submit Monthly Highlights Report form	2. Provide mini-performance feedback sessions for each direct report. Use the DMAIC, AAR, and project management format	2. Provide performance feedback sessions for each direct report. Use the DMAIC, AAR, and project management format
	3. Complete or review and analyze quality audit requirements		3. Establish rolling monthly agenda and conduct monthly meeting with plant manager team—use the DMAIC, AAR, and project management format		3. Revisit or redevelop strategic plan, and develop alignment with KPIs and goals

	Daily	Weekly	Monthly	Annual
	4. Establish proactive agenda items for the daily shift or team meeting	4. Document organization wide performance and outlook document or communication		4. Document organization-wide performance and outlook document or communication
	5. Look for and facilitate CI opportunities to be logged on CI worksheet			5. Attend annual organizational performance meetings
	6. Process and people problem solve as needed			6. Complete and submit Annual Highlights Report form
	7. Communicate once per day with next level (both up and down) leadership.			
Plant manager	1. Follow appropriate work instructions and procedures, and complete job description activities	1. Daily activities plus the following	1. Review all Plant level KPIs, goals, and individual subordinate performance. Check for alignment with organization strategy. Modify as needed	1. Weekly activities plus the following
				1. Review all plant level KPIs, goals, and individual subordinate performance. Check for alignment with organization strategy. Modify as needed

(Continued)

(Continued)

	Daily	Weekly	Monthly	Semi-Annually	Annually
	2. Complete and analyze required productivity reports, including hour reports and job reporting—plant-level data.	2. Establish rolling weekly agenda and conduct weekly meeting with each department/ area manager—use the DMAIC, After AAR, and project management format	2. Complete and submit Monthly Highlights Report form	2. Provide mini-performance feedback sessions for each direct report. Use the DMAIC, AAR, and project management format	2. Provide performance feedback sessions for each direct report. Use the DMAIC, AAR, and project management format
	3. Complete or review and analyze quality audit requirements		3. Establish rolling monthly agenda and conduct monthly meeting with department/ area manager team—use the DMAIC, AAR, and project management format		3. Revisit or redevelop strategic plan, and develop alignment with KPIs and goals
	4. Establish proactive agenda items for the daily shift or team meeting		4. Deliver organization-wide performance and outlook document or communication		4. Document organization wide performance and outlook document or communication
	5. Look for and facilitate CI opportunities to be logged on CI worksheet				5. Attend annual organizational performance meetings

	6. Process and people problem solve as needed 7. Communicate once per day with next level (both up and down) leadership				6. Complete and submit Annual Highlights Report form
Department, area, or value stream manager	1. Follow appropriate work instructions and procedures, and complete job description activities 2. Complete and analyze required productivity reports, including hour reports and job reporting—department/area-level data 3. Complete or review and analyze quality audit requirements	1. Daily activities plus the following 2. Establish rolling weekly agenda and conduct weekly meeting with each department/area supervisor—use the DMAIC, AAR, and project management format	1. Weekly activities plus the following 2. Complete and submit monthly highlights report form 3. Establish rolling monthly agenda and conduct monthly meeting with department/area supervisor team—use the DMAIC, AAR, and project management format	1. Review all department or area level KPIs, goals, and individual subordinate performance. Check for alignment with plant strategy. Modify as needed 2. Provide mini-performance feedback sessions for each direct report. Use the DMAIC, AAR, and project management format	1. Attend annual organizational performance meetings 2. Complete and submit Annual Highlights Report form 3. Revisit or recommit to the strategic plan, and understand alignment with KPIs and goals

(Continued)

(Continued)

	Daily	Weekly	Monthly	Semi-Annually	Annually
	4. Establish proactive agenda items for the daily shift or team meeting		4. Deliver organization wide performance and outlook document or communication		4. Deliver organization-wide performance and outlook document or communication
	5. Look for and facilitate CI opportunities to be logged on CI worksheet				5. Review all department/area level KPIs, goals, and individual subordinate performance. Check for alignment with organization strategy. Modify as needed
	6. Process and people problem solve as needed				6. Provide performance feedback sessions for each direct report. Use the DMAIC, AAR, and project management format
	7. Communicate once per day with next level (both up and down) leadership				
Department or area supervisor	1. Follow supervisor work instructions and procedures, and complete job description activities	1. Daily activities plus the following	1. Weekly activities plus the following	1. Review all department/area level KPIs, goals, and individual subordinate performance. Check for alignment with plant strategy. Modify as needed	1. Attend annual organizational performance meetings

2. Complete supervisor productivity reports, including hour reports and job reporting	2. Establish rolling weekly agenda and conduct weekly meeting with each WTL—use the DMAIC, AAR, and project management format	2. Complete and submit monthly highlights report form	2. Provide mini-performance feedback sessions for each direct report. Use the DMAIC, AAR, and project management format	2. Complete and submit Annual Highlights Report form
3. Complete quality audit requirements		3. Establish rolling monthly agenda and conduct monthly meeting with WTL team—Use the DMAIC, AAR, and project management format.		3. Revisit or recommit to the strategic plan, and understand alignment with KPIs and goals
4. Establish proactive agenda items for, and attend and/or co-lead daily shift or team meeting		4. Deliver organization wide performance and outlook document or communication		4. Deliver organization-wide performance and outlook document or communication
5. Look for and facilitate CI opportunities to be logged on CI worksheet				5. Review all department/area level KPIs, goals, and individual subordinate performance. Check for alignment with organization strategy. Modify as needed

(Continued)

(Continued)

	Daily	Weekly	Monthly	Semi-Annually	Annually
Work team leader (WTL)	6. Process and people problem solve as needed				6. Provide performance feedback sessions for each direct report. Use the DMAIC, AAR, and project management format
	1. Follow WTL work instructions and procedures, and complete Job Description activities	1. Daily activities plus the following	1. Weekly activities plus the following	1. Review all work team level KPIs, goals, and individual subordinate performance. Check for alignment with department or area strategy. Modify as needed	1. Attend annual organizational performance meetings
	2. Complete work team productivity reports, including hour reports and job reporting		2. Complete and submit monthly highlights report form	2. Provide mini-performance feedback sessions for each direct report. Use the DMAIC, AAR, and project management format	2. Complete and submit Annual Highlights Report form
	3. Complete quality audit requirements		3. Establish rolling monthly agenda and conduct monthly meeting with work teams—use the DMAIC, AAR, and project management format		3. Revisit or recommit to the strategic plan, and understand alignment with KPIs and goals.

4. Lead daily shift or team meeting	4. Deliver organization wide performance and outlook document or communication	4. Deliver organization-wide performance and outlook document or communication
5. Look for and facilitate CI opportunities to be logged on CI worksheet		5. Review all work team level KPIs, goals, and individual subordinate performance. Check for alignment with organization strategy. Modify as needed
6. Process and people problem solve as needed		6. Provide performance feedback sessions for each direct report. Use the DMAIC, AAR, and project management format

Concluding, Larry added, "Much of leader standard work is defined by Mark Harnish in his book *Mastering the Rockefeller Habits* as 'meeting rhythms.' Meeting rhythms for us include daily team huddles, weekly cross-functional planning sessions, and monthly performance review sessions. Each session has standard agendas and objectives."

"Tell me more about the standard agendas," coaxed Joe.

Larry continued, "Well, our standard agendas are basically the same. At each session the group looks at what has happened since the last session versus what was the plan, and then they review or initiate corrective and/or preventative actions, discuss any outstanding individual or team performance to recognize, and then they cover what should happen between now and the next session."

Larry walked Joe over to another chart on the wall and explained the details. "Here is the standard agenda for the daily huddle sessions."

Daily Huddle Standard Agenda

Number	Topic	Time
1	What happened yesterday versus what was supposed to happen? Performance and action item followup	3–4 minutes
2	What do the daily metrics indicate? Did we achieve the goals? If not why not?	3–4 minutes
3	What do we need to do today (or this shift) to correct or prevent problems? Who will do what, by when?	3–5 minutes
4	Who are the outstanding performers, what did they do, and how did it help?	1–2 minutes
5	Adjourn	10–15 minutes total

Attendees: All team members Leader: team leader

"Each day at the designated time, the area team leader leads a team huddle with the entire team at the area dashboard, and works through the standard agenda." explained Larry.

Weekly Cross-functional Work Session Standard Agenda

Number	Topic	Time
1	What happened last week versus what was supposed to happen? Performance and action item follow-up	8–18 minutes

Weekly Cross-functional Work Session Standard Agenda (Continued)

Number	Topic	Time
2	What do the weekly metrics indicate? Did we achieve the goals? If not why not?	8–18 minutes
3	What do we need to do this week to correct or prevent problems? Who will do what, by when?	8–18 minutes
4	Who are the outstanding performers, what did they do, and how did it help?	~6 minutes
5	Adjourn	30–60 minutes total

Attendees: Cross-functional leaders: Operation manager

Monthly Performance Work Session Standard Agenda

Number	Topic	Time
1	What happened last month versus what was supposed to happen? Performance and action item follow-up.	8–18 minutes
2	What do the monthly metrics indicate? Did we achieve the goals? If not why not?	8–18 minutes
3	What do we need to do this month to correct or prevent problems? Who will do what, by when?	8–18 minutes
4	Who are the outstanding performers, what did they do, and how did it help?	~ 6 minutes
5	Adjourn	30–60 minutes total

Attendees: Area managers and executives. Leader: CEO

"On a weekly basis," continued Larry, "the operations manager leads the weekly cross-functional work session in the conference room we started in. And then, on a monthly basis, the CEO leads the monthly performance work session with all the area managers and executives. Of course, each organization has to adapt the standard work to their specific needs. Additionally, once per quarter the CEO leads an organization-wide meeting where she and the other leaders discuss the organization's mission, vision, and values, as well as explain what's going on with the organization and our customers. It's very informative, and it's all driven from our daily, weekly, and monthly scorecards and dashboards."

"What's the difference between your scorecards and dashboards?" asked Joe.

"They are similar but different," replied Larry. "Scorecards are where we keep the score, like in golf or bowling. Depending on the area, some areas share the workload of completing the scorecards, and have different people fill in their daily scorecards just before the daily huddles, other area scorecards are populated by the team leaders. In either case the scorecards are completed for yesterdays, or the last shifts work, before the huddle session."

Larry continued, "Dashboards are where scorecard data are graphically displayed so historical trends can be seen and analyzed more easily. It is like if you were trying to lose weight, you'd weigh yourself every day and jot down your weight on a scorecard, and then at the end of the week, you'd plot the scorecard data on a graph to see the trend. Dashboards typically are more graphically driven, and show trends better; just like we learned in class. I'll show you an example when we get to the display areas."

"Okay," said Joe, "but when the standard agenda indicates '*What do we need to do today (this week or this month) to correct or prevent problems? Who will do what, by when?*' What do you actually do?"

"It depends," replied Larry. "On a daily basis it may just be who will talk to whom, and nothing much is formally documented except for what is on the scorecard white board. However, if the issue is big enough, we'll initiate an A3."

"Now you've lost me, what's an A3?" said Joe.

Larry laughed and replied, "I know, 'A3' is a silly name, but an A3 is simply a problem solving or improvement tracking tool. The term A3 actually comes from the Avery paper size of A3, which is actually about the same as an 11" × 17" page. This paper size allows for a single page to be used to document a problem resolution or improvement project. What you'll see on our dashboards is that the problem or target improvement area graphs are tagged with an A3 note, and the actual A3 is posted below on the same dashboard. That way, when we're conducting the work session, we can look at the A3 at the same time, or anyone walking by the dashboard can quickly see the status of the improvement or problem-solving effort. It really makes it easy to manage problem solving and improvements. Here is a blank A3 for you," and Larry handed Joe an 11" × 17" page shown as follows:

Or

Source: MCS MEDIA, 888 RIDGE RD., CHELSEA, MI 48118.

"Once we initiate an A3 we use the basic Lean and Six Sigma tools to identify root causes, and implement improvements. The basic metrics management process is illustrated on our information boards. Take a look at this." Larry said as he pointed to the following diagram.

The "path to excellecnce" leadership system

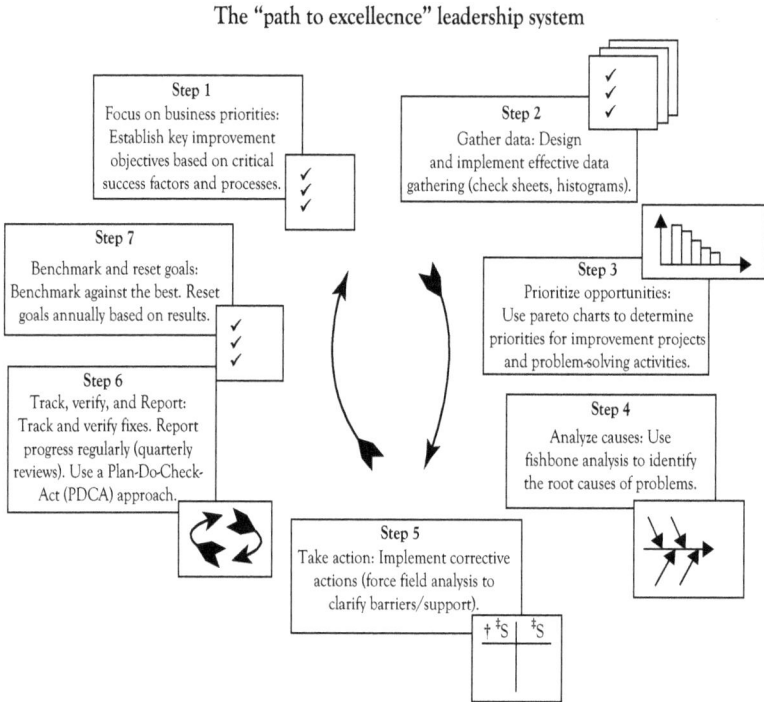

Source: PMIC consulting Bill Guest, President and CSA at Metrics Reporting, Inc.

The Seven Steps:

1. FOCUS on business priorities: Establish key improvement objectives based on critical success factors, KPIs, and processes.

2. Gather DATA: Design and implement effective data gathering (check sheets, histograms).

3. PRIORITIZE opportunities: Use Pareto charts to determine priorities for improvement projects and problem-solving activities.

4. ANALYZE causes: Use fishbone analysis to identify the root causes of problems.

5. Take ACTION: Implement corrective actions (force field analysis to clarify barriers/support).

6. Track, verify, and REPORT: Track and verify fixes. Report progress regularly (quarterly reviews). Use a Plan-Do-Check-Act (PDCA) approach.

7. BENCHMARK and reset goals: Benchmark against the best. Reset goals annually based on results.

The following is an eight-step checklist to help you get started to maximizing your organization's resources through a systematic approach to leadership. This process works for every level of an organization.

1. Establish the 7–10 key improvement objectives for the organization or area.
2. Assign key leaders in the organization to each lead one of the objectives.
3. Using Pareto charts, determine the top three or four problems for each objective (80/20 rule).
4. Note: 7–10 objectives, with three or four problems each, results in a total list of about 21–40 problems.
5. Assign project teams (three to five members) to each problem for analysis and corrective action.
6. Require the project team leaders to hold weekly meetings to insure progress on each project.
7. Hold quarterly for decisions and accountability on each of the projects.
8. Require the key objective leaders to bench mark and set new goals each year.

Note: The projects do not all need to be active at the same time. If resources are limited, assign projects for each objective one or two at a time. After a few months, kick off the next project with the goal to complete all 25 within a year.

The light went on for Joe. The A3 and the leadership process were the missing components from his system. He couldn't wait to get back to work. Joe finished the short walk-through with Larry, and hustled back to work to meet with his leaders.

Joe reviewed what he had learned with his team leaders, and they agreed to initiate an A3 for the scrap and rework issue. They stared with a problem statement that the delivery performance was poor and completed a brief 5-Why analysis. It went like this.

Problem statement: Delivery performance to the customer is below goal.

Why 1 = Why is the delivery performance to the customer below goal?

Answer 1 = Our schedule attainment is below goal, and if we do not meet our schedule, we will not be on time to our customers.

Why 2 = Why is our schedule attainment below goal?

Answer 2 = We have to rework and scrap too many parts. If we have to rework or scrap parts we have to make more parts to fulfill the quantity requirements. Our schedules do not account for running extra parts or the time to rework.

Why 3 = Why do we have to rework or scrap too many parts?

Answer 3 = Parts are being produced with defects.

Why 4 = Why are parts being produced with defects?

Answer 4 = The machine malfunctions periodically producing a defective part.

Why 5 = Why is the machine malfunctioning?

Answer 5 = We are not sure and need to investigate. It could be due to lack of preventative maintenance, electrical or controls problems, or machine wear, or another issue. This is the enhanced problem statement we will start the A3 with concluded Joe.

The team completed the following A3, and Joe and the team leaders established standard work similar to what Joe had seen at Supply Chain Inc.

In a few short weeks and several problem-solving sessions, the team discovered that a worn machine part was causing the machine to malfunction periodically, and make a defective part. The team had the defective machine part replaced and established a statistical control chart to monitor the process and ensure that they would be able to identify when the machine part was beginning to wear. This would allow them to prevent future defects from occurring due to that part being worn put again.

Joe began to post weekly trend charts on a dashboard, and the team could see the impact they were having on the process. Not only were the rework and scrap numbers being brought under goals, but the schedule attainment and on time delivery to the customer numbers were improving as well.

A3 Project Planner/Tracker: **Project Name:**

1. Problem Statement and or Improvement Charter

Original problem statement: Delivery performance to the customer is below goal.

Why 1 = Why is the delivery performance to the customer below goal?
Answer 1 = Our schedule attainment is below goal, and if we do not meet our schedule, we will not be on time to our customers.

Why 2 = Why is our schedule attainment below goal?
Answer 2 = We have to rework and scrap too many parts. If we have to rework or scrap parts we have to make more parts to fulfill the quantity requirements. Our schedules do not account for running extra parts or the time to rework.

Why 3 = Why do we have to rework or scrap too many parts?
Answer = Parts are being produced with defects.

Why 4 = Why are parts being produced with defects?
Answer = The machine malfunctions periodically producing a defective part.

Why 5 = Why is the machine malfunctioning?

Answer = We are not sure and need to investigate. It could be due to lack of preventative maintenance, electrical or controls problems, or machine wear, or another issue.

5. Future State

Replace the defective machine part

Develop a Preventative and Productive Maintenance (PM) plan to maintain and detect machine wear more proactively.

6. Future Opportunities
1. How can we let our machines deteriorate so badly before we do something about it?
2. How can we proactively determine the cause and effect relationships?
3. Maybe we need a layered audit system to maintain our PM system?

3. Current State

Daily on-time in full deliveries to schedule (OTIF)

1. Machine problems are causing excessive scrap and poor schedule attainment, which leads to poor delivery.
2. Improve machine problems and we should reduce scrap, and get back to acceptable schedule attainment.

4. Issues and Opportunities
1. We need to improve customer relationships. They are getting upset with us missing dates.

7. Implementation Plan and Time-line

	Action Items and Tasks	Status/Comments	% Comp		Dates
1	Establish the team	Complete	100%	JM	19-Aug
2	Conduct the kick-off session and set goals	Complete	100%	JM	10-Aug
3	Define the problem, issues and opportunities	Complete	100%	JM	10-Aug
4	Measure and collect process data	Complete	100%	TL	17-Aug
5	Analyse data	Complete	100%	BJ	24-Aug
6	Develop improvement action items	Complete	100%	GH	1-Sep
7	Implement improvement action items	Complete	100%	MN	16-Sep
8	Replace defective machine part and measure impact	Complete	100%	KP	1-Oct
9	Develop a PM plan	Complete	100%	PD	15-Oct
10	Implement the PM plan	Complete	100%	KP	15-Oct
11	Verify corrective action with data	In progress	100%	JQ	15-Oct
12	Sustain the PM system	On-going	50%	TL	31-Oct
13	Monitor and improve the OTD metric	On-going		OP	
14	Congratulate the team success			OP	

8. Outcome Measures

	Measures	Current			After Implementation	
1	Customer On time delivery (OTD)	Below goal	90%	average	At Goal	100%
2	Schedule Attainment	Below Goal	92%	average	At Goal	100%
	See charts on this report					

Team: Leader: JM   Team: OP, TL, JQ, KP, PD, MN

After several weeks of tracking daily measures, and making slight adjustments to the key measures tracking sheet and process, the teams were really beginning to excel. The work areas were monitoring their own key measures and responding to them accordingly to improve performance. They felt more knowledgeable about overall organizational performance, as well as their own. People went home everyday feeling a sense of accomplishment and success, or with a desire to make improvements in efforts or take countermeasures for improving the next day.

A color-coded visual representation of their daily scorecard is shown as follows:

Joe began to see some trends and connections or correlations between some of the measures. For example, Joe noticed that the more rework and scrap they had, the more they missed schedule attainment, and the more they missed schedule attainment, the more they missed deliveries to the customer. Everyone intuitively knew this, but the data was very

Daily Operations Scorecard

	Measure	Goals	2-Aug	3-Aug	4-Aug	5-Aug	6-Aug	7-Aug	8-Aug	9-Aug	10-Aug	11-Aug	12-Aug	13-Aug	14-Aug	15-Aug	16-Aug	17-Aug	18-Aug	19-Aug	20-Aug	21-Aug	22-Aug	23-Aug	24-Aug	25-Aug	26-Aug	27-Aug	28-Aug	29-Aug	30-Aug	31-Aug
People	Attendance Percent	100%	100%	100%	100%	100%	99%	100%	100%	100%	100%																					
	Consecutive Days Safe	Increase	123	124	125	126	127	128	129	130																						
Delivery	Daily on-time or full deliveries to schedule (DIFF)	100%	100%	99%	100%	100%	44%	98%	98%	98%																						
	Daily schedule attainment	100%	91%	90%	82%	90%	64%	64%	100%	99%																						
	Less Than Lead time (LTLT) orders achieved as a percent of total LTLT orders taken	100%	100%	100%	99%	99%	76%	84%	99%	100%																						
Quality	Scrap pieces per day	<15	12	26	18	13	22	34	13																							
	Rejected units per day	0	0	1	0	2	0	0	0	0																						
Productivity	Standard hours per day	>100%	100%	99%	100%	98%	100%	100%	115%																							
	Actual units per person per day versus scheduled units per person per day	0	0	0	3	0	0	10	2																							
	Block outs per day	<15%	14.79%	20.50%	18.50%	11%	12%	16%	41%	6.7%																						
Customer	Customer return dollars	$0	$122	$0	$0	$60	$0	$0	$0																							
	Customer complaints	0	1	0	0	0	0	1	0																							
Financial	Bonus status	Yes	Yes	Yes	Yes	Yes	Yes	Yes	Yes	Yes																						
	Sales dollars shipped	>$32K	$24,000	$25,000	$35,000	$36,000	$42,000	$95,000	$225,000	$36,000																						

Daily Operations Dashboard

FINANCIAL

Sales dollars shipped
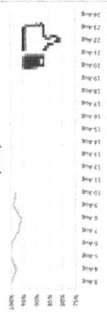

CUSTOMER

Customer return dollars
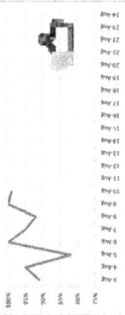

Customer complaints

PRODUCTIVITY

Actual units per person per day versus scheduled units per person per day
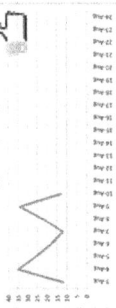

Stock outs per day

Labor cost percent of sales
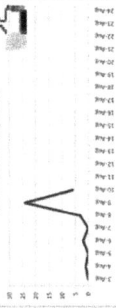

QUALITY

Scrap pieces per day
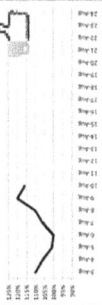

Rejected units per day
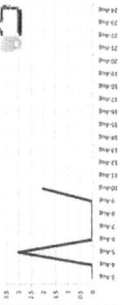

Reworked items per day
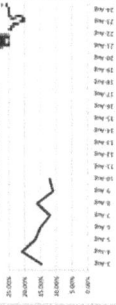

DELIVERY

Daily on-time in full deliveries to schedule (OTIF)
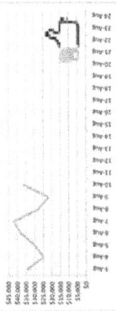

Daily schedule attainment
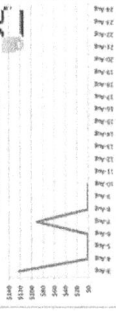

Less Than Lead time (LTLT) orders achieved as a percent of total LTLT orders taken.
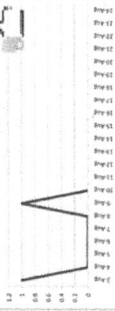

PEOPLE

Consecutive Days Safe
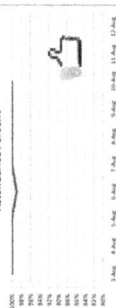

Attendance Percent
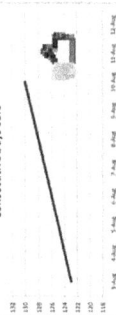

BONUS

compelling. Through these observed connections, Joe and the production groups were able to focus their improvement efforts on the vital few indicators that drove overall success.

The previous figure is the daily trend charts Joe posted from the Scorecard data shown earlier.

Joe's job got easier as well. He was no longer a slave to data collection and computer work. As he made his rounds, the teams seemed to be working on the right things. The teams were knowledgeable of the status of the organization, and they knew what their role and responsibility was for improvement. They knew the score! Joe only had to ask about exceptions, and special projects, and clear the way for the teams to succeed.

Joe became more of a supportive leader. Eventually he accepted a promotion to operations manager. Nice work Joe! Way to keep score!

Discussion Questions

1. Has your organization implemented an hour-by-hour scoreboard? If yes, how does it compare with the one Joe has created? If no, do you see a value in one and how would you go about implementing it?

2. Do you agree with the statement, "You see every person in our organization, from the CEO to the first-level supervisor, every leader, and every person has standard work?" Does your organization have standard work defined for the middle to upper management? Explain.

3. Do you think it is a good idea to have standard agendas and objectives for the daily huddle sessions, weekly cross-functional planning sessions, and monthly performance review sessions? Does your organization follow this practice?

4. Discuss the basic metrics management process outlined in this chapter. Does your organization have a similar process in place? What process does your organization follow to identify root causes and implement improvements?

5. Does your organization do a good job in studying the relationship between different performance measures? Do you think it is beneficial for your organization to do so?

CHAPTER 8

Making Cultural Transitions

Joe was showing such great improvements in operations that he finally got the attention of the senior management team. The management team invited Joe to an upcoming session and asked him to deliver a short presentation on his scorecard and dashboard systems. Joe was excited about the opportunity to present his new system, and to show his success.

In preparation for the session, Joe compiled monthly scorecard data for operations and created dashboard for the year to date, as shown on the pages 72–73:

With the scorecard data and the dashboard charts, Joe was able to explain in great detail what was happening in the operations area, and what his next step for improvement was going to be. The senior management team asked a lot of questions regarding the indicators that were showing the "thumbs down" visual signal.

Joe took the time to explain and comment on each metric to make sure everyone understood why the thumb was up or down.

Joe explained, "Our one financial measure is sales per month, and is something that we in operations have little control over, yet it's this demand that drives all of our work, and many of our productivity measures, so we track it and show our people how the trends are going so they know what to expect. So far this year sales has been meeting goal for the most part. In March, there was a significant drop in sales due to the unplanned shut down of one of our major customers."

"Our customer metrics are customer return dollars and customer complaints. Customer return dollars has been on a steady decline since April, and this is a great trend. I congratulated the team on their efforts in this area."

"Customer complaints are below goal and holding fairly steady, however, we still have some work to do here. As you know, we track and have

Monthly Operations Scorecard

	Measure	Goals	JAN	FEB	MAR	APR	MAY	JUN	JUL	AUG	SEP	OCT	NOV	DEC
People	Attendance Percent	>99.75%	99.34%	99.68%	99.89%	99.78%	99.85%	99.57%	99.76%	99.86%				
	Consecutive Days Safe	Increase	160	191	221	28	59	89	120	151				
Delivery	On-time in full deliveries to schedule (OTIF)	>98.50%	98.90%	99.00%	97.80%	98.70%	98.90%	99.25%	98.90%	99.27%				
	Schedule attainment	>95%	96.00%	98.00%	89.00%	90.00%	93.00%	98.00%	94.00%	97.14%				
	Less Than Lead time (LTLT) orders achieved as a percent of total LTLT orders taken.	>98.5%	99.00%	98.00%	99.50%	99.90%	99.75%	98.50%	98.75%	99.90%				
Quality	Scrap pieces per month	<450	400	389	365	435	445	434	456	323				
	Rejected units per month	≤5	5	2	4	3	5	4	5	6				
	Reworked items per month	<100	56	76	85	78	87	56	98	78				
Productivity	Actual units per person versus scheduled units per person monthly	≥100%	98%	112%	107%	111%	109%	100%	99%	105%				
	Stock outs per month	≤5	3	2	4	5	2	3	4	6				
	Labor cost percent of sales	<15%	14.76%	12.87%	16.52%	13.13%	14.68%	13.98%	12.99%	13.69%				
Customer	Customer return dollars	<$500	$454	$332	$255	$455	$435	$395	$350	$234				
	Customer complaints	≤5	4	3	2	5	4	2	3	3				
Financial	Bonus status	Yes	Yes	Yes	No	Yes	Yes	Yes	Yes	Yes				
	Sales dollars shipped	>$900K	$921,000	$915,000	$775,000	$902,000	$914,000	$899,000	$910,000	$907,000				

Monthly Operations Dashboard

a formal corrective action for every customer complaint. I'm optimistic about upcoming months."

"Our productivity measures are actual units per person versus scheduled units per person, stock outs, and labor cost as a percent of sales. Our units per person metric are starting to turn the corner and show an improving trend since last month. Our labor cost to sales is holding steady just below goal, but our stock out have been increasing at an alarming rate. This is mainly due to one source, and we are working with purchasing to resource the components we buy from the problem supplier. Since we've been considering resourcing, the current supplier's performance has gotten worse. We need to make this change as soon as possible and before stock outs begin to affect our delivery performance."

"Our quality metrics are scrap parts, rejected units, and reworked items. There is good news and bad news with the quality metrics. While we believe the scrap is now under control and will continue to decline, we are seeing more units rejected and reworked over the past several months. This is good in that we are not shipping defective units to the customer, but we need to determine the root cause of the problems and get them fixed. We have initiated an A3 improvement project to get to the bottom of this, and we expect their improvements to take effect beginning next month. We are using a plan, do, check, act improvement methodology, and must take the time to validate our improvements."

"Our delivery key measures are on-time and full shipments, schedule attainment, and less than lead time (LTLT) orders shipped on time. Our customers really take advantage of our LTLT order plan, and we make extra money from this service. Our sales team claims it not only gets us more orders, but it increases our profitability, and we are getting better at meeting the commitments. We found that our poor schedule attainment was due to a machine problem which is now fixed through an A3 improvement team's efforts. Once the machine improvement took place, our scrap, and rework numbers improved, and we were able to attain our planned schedule. Once we started to hit the schedule, our on-time delivery (OTD) also improved. It was a true cause and effect relationship, and our delivery numbers are all improving."

"Lastly, our people measures are attendance, consecutive days safe, and our bonus attainment. For the bonus attainment we simply show a big 'thumbs up' if we are getting a bonus. Our people are really driven by this as you can imagine. The key is to make sure they know that it is by achieving the goals on all the other metrics that leads to us getting a bonus. Attendance has been holding steady as well. There are no significant issues there. As you can see we had an accident in April this year when Tom Jenkins in production cut his finger and had to go to the medical center for stitches. Since then, we've been accident free, and are back on track for a new record again. Since Tom's injury we have upgraded our gloves, and we would expect to avoid his type of injury in the future."

"That's all I have on the dashboard numbers, any questions?" concluded Joe.

Joe answered a few questions regarding the data, A3s, and next steps, and then the president spoke up.

"Joe, this is nice work. How are the people feeling about the scorecards and dashboards?" inquired Mr. Helmsly.

"The people love them!" replied Joe emphatically. "Now they know just where they stand on a daily basis. They go home after their shift knowing if they've won or lost for the day. They've also indicated to me that they know, just what to do to improve, and how to set priorities without me getting involved in every decision. This has freed me up to lead more improvement and cost-saving activities. Overall, it's been a very powerful tool, and has shifted our culture to one of

- Shared knowledge and competency
- Data and goal-driven productivity, quality, speed, and efficiency
- Bias for improvement and prevention actions and measured results
- Improved communications and focus
- Common goals and team work
- Improved decision making
- Self-motivated accomplishment and achievement

As long as I don't use the metrics to 'beat people up,' it works great for everyone. It was really that simple."

Mr. Helmsly prodded more, "One more thing Joe, do you think this would work for my management team?" he said with a smirk as he glanced around the table.

Joe hesitated briefly and replied, "I'm certain it would Mr. Helmsly, and I'd be willing to help anyone interested in implementing this process."

"That's the right answer Joe, and please stop calling me Mr. Helmsly. You can call me Jack." Mr. Helmsly replied.

Joe smiled and said, "Thanks Jack."

And with that, Mr. Helmsly instructed each member of his management team to work with Joe to establish scorecards and dashboards for their next session, and adjourned the meeting.

Discussion Questions

1. Critically evaluate Joe's presentation to the management team. If you were Joe, would you have done anything differently?
2. What lessons can an organization that is planning to implement scorecards and dashboards learn from Joe's presentation and the process he used?
3. Do you agree with the cultural shifts that have occurred on account of Joe's implementation of dashboards and scorecards in his organization? If so, shouldn't all organizations do the same?

CHAPTER 9

Achieving, Sustaining, and Celebrating Success

Larry and Joe had not seen each other for several months when they arrived at the gym for a scrimmage game before the next basketball season.

"Hey Joe," shouted Larry. "How's the defending champion doing?"

"Sounds like you've finally gotten over the championship game," replied Joe.

"Well not really, but I have a feeling this is our year, we just hired a 6'3" sales team manager," boasted Larry.

"Yeah, but can he play?" asked Joe.

"Can *SHE* play?" replied Larry, "She's the state female player of the year for four straight years from Janesville High School. She not only can play, she led the Janesville High School Lady Hawks to three consecutive state championships, before playing college ball at state. She can play; and she is playing for us this year!" said Larry excitedly.

"Well we're still defending champs," replied Joe.

"If the lights stay on this year, you won't have a chance. Speaking of the lights coming on, how's your improvement effort going? Did you finally see the light?" continued Larry.

"It's going great," said Joe. "Jack even asked me to help the management team."

"Jack? Mr. Helmsly?" asked Larry.

"Yeah, he asked me to call him Jack. I guess I'm in the inner circle," replied Joe. "Do you have any advice for handling the management team?" asked Joe.

"Well to manage and sustain improvement leaders must learn to understand and manage change," said Larry. "People will get nervous during times of change and improvement. We always stick to and reinforce the basics to help our teams cope with improvements and change. It's important to show your commitment. Remember the key enablers? Ask yourself what, if anything is missing?" Larry added.

Key Enablers for Lean Sigma Success

1. Leadership establishing, communicating, and living up to the vision, mission, and values
2. Resource commitment
3. Training and education
4. Process and results focused
5. Policy deployment and goal alignment
6. Total system or value stream focus
7. Employee involvement
8. Perseverance and commitment

Source: Rob Ptacek and Jaideep Motwani, Pursuing Perfect Service (Michigan, MI: MCS Media, Inc., 2011). James Womack and Daniel Jones, Lean Thinking (London, England: Productiviy Press, 1996)

Larry continued, "We also try to come up with some new challenges or themes to keep things fresh. If everything is going well, we'll focus on one key metric to improve, like customer focus or quality. We'll ask each team to come up with ideas for improvement. We may even run a contest for the best idea or something like that to keep things alive." One time when we set new goals for customer satisfaction, someone came up with an idea for an open house for our customers. The customers were invited to attend a couple free training courses on continuous improvement and sustainability. We also invited in a couple local government officials in to speak. It was very successful, not only did our customers appreciate the free leaning opportunities; we had a chance to show off our systems."

Larry continued, "We then created another theme to push accomplishment even farther. We created a competition within the organization, and the winning team with the most improvements would get their car washed by the management team. Again we had a lot of fun with this.

It took about a year to achieve the goal, but we succeeded in raising the bar of achievement. You might try a theme or a challenge, or internal competition to get some excitement back into the improvement effort."

"When you're managing improvement and change in an organization, things can get difficult," continued Larry. Larry sketched the following illustration on the whiteboard in the locker room, and explained. "You see, at first, once everyone sees that you're serious about improving, and gets over the shock and denial, people begin to see how the Lean Sigma improvements can help them. They start to see some quick hitting improvements, and are optimistic. Then, when the 'low hanging fruit' or easy projects have been implemented, things get tougher, and improvements are harder to find. When this happens, things start to plateau or level out. If left alone, this plateau will turn into pessimism and doubt. At this point people need to see management's commitment to improvement methods. Too many leaders throw in the towel at this point, and go back to their old ways.

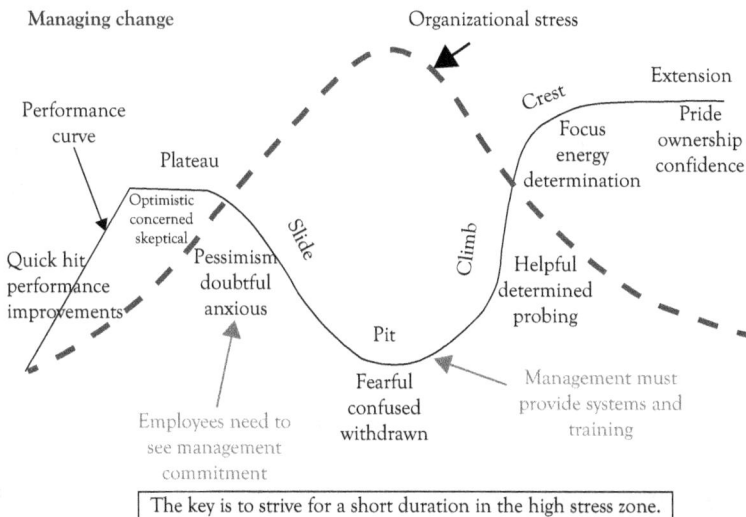

If managers and leaders redouble their efforts and commitments at this point, things will start to turn around, and many more significant gains will occur. The key is to push through the trough or 'organizational stress' as quickly as possible, by sticking to key projects and a systematic or stand method of leadership."

Joe said, "That's interesting, but I think we are beyond that now, and I just want to get some more excitement around the shop. I think a challenge, something big, will be a good way to get the excitement back."

"In Jim Collins' book *Good to Great,* he called them 'Big Hairy Audacious Goals' or BHAGs, and many organizations have them. They provide long-term focus and can be fun," Larry added.

"Another key is to continue to hold people accountable to use the scorecard and dashboard methods and tools. This should be built right into your performance management system. Keep to the accountability sessions or 'Meeting Rhythms' as Harnish called them in his book *Mastering the Rockefeller Habits.* In the book, Harnish describes a meeting rhythm with daily huddles, weekly, monthly, and quarterly work sessions to review progress to goals, ensure resources are provided, and to hold people and teams accountable for results. This is a key to sustaining the effort. Remember the standard work for leaders we discussed? Make these work sessions standard work for you and your area leaders. Perform layered process audits to make sure they are doing them, and doing them correctly. This will let the teams see that these are important to you, and to their success." Larry added.

"Boy, sustaining the effort can hard work!" said Joe.

"Not as hard as it will be to repeat as league champs! You won the championship game in the dark, you we're in the dark at your company, and now I leave you in the dark again!" said Larry as he turned the locker room lights off and ducked out of the door.

Discussion Questions

1. Do you agree with Larry's statement, "We always go back to the basics to recharge our team?" Why do you think it is important to go back to the basics? Do you think that the key enablers identified earlier in the book were the right ones? Why or why not?

2. Is it a good idea to create a competition within the organization on which functional area comes up with the most improvements? Will such a competition raise the bar or will it create more conflicts? What do you think of Larry's reward to the team that won this competition?

3. Discuss the change cycle presented by Larry. Why is it difficult to implement change in any organization?
4. What do you think of Joe's statement on how to get more excitement in the shop? What lessons can Joe learn from Jim Collins' book?
5. Why is it critical for an organization to hold people accountable for the use of standardized leadership methods and tools?
6. If you were Joe, what are the five things that you would emphasize in order to sustain the success and momentum achieved from implementing scorecards and dashboards?

References

Collins, J. C. (2001). *Good to great: Why some companies make the leap-and others don't.* New York, NY: Harper Business.

Covey, S. (1997). *The seven habits of highly effective people: Restoring the character ethic.* Boston, MA: G K Hall & Co.

Gitomer, J. (1998). *Customer satisfaction is worthless; customer loyalty is priceless.* Austin, TX: Bard Press.

Harnish, V. (2002). *Mastering the rockefeller habits: What you must do to increase the value of your growing firm* (Ist ed.). Las Vegas, NV: Gazelles, Inc.

Liker, J.K. (2004). *The Toyota way: 14 management principles from the world's greatest manufacturer.* New York, NY: McGraw-Hill.

Liker, J.K. (2008). *Toyota culture: The heart and soul of the Toyota way.* New York, NY: McGraw-Hill.

Lundin, S., Paul, H., &Christensen, J. (2000). *Fish! A proven way to boost morale and improve results* (Ist ed.). Santa Clara, CA: Hyperion.

Ptacek, R., Coats, M., & Ptacek, T. (2012). *Today's Lean leader! A practical guide to applying Lean Six Sigma and emerging technologies to leadership and supervision.* Chelsea, MI: MCS Media, Inc.

Ptacek, R., & Motwani, J. (2011a). *Pursuing perfect service – Using a practical approach to Lean Six Sigma to improve the customer experience and reduce costs in service industries.* Chelsea, MI: MCS Media, Inc.

Ptacek, R., & Motwani, J. (2011b). *The Lean Six Sigma pocket guide XL – combining the best of both worlds together to eliminate waste.* Chelsea, MI: MCS Media, Inc.

Spear, S., & Bowen, H.K. (1999, September). Decoding the DNA of the Toyota production system. *Harvard Business Review.*

Spear, S. (1999, May). Learning to lead at Toyota. *Harvard Business Review.* 1–9.

Womack, J.P., & Jones, D.T. (1996). *Lean thinking: Banish waste and create wealth in your organization.* New York, NY: Simon and Schuster.

Suggestions for further reading

Strategy: Sun Tzu, Ansoff, Porter, Ohmae

Management: Taylor, Barnard, Drucker, Kepner/Tregoe, Peters, Covey, Collins

Quality: Crosby, Deming, Juran, Shingo

Leadership: Carnegie, Follett, Maslow, Herzberg, McGregor, Hersey, Blanchard
Change: Kanter, Schein, Hammer
Marketing: Levitt, Kotler

Measurement: Kaplan/Norton, Brown, Niven

Trends: Toffler, Naisbitt, Handy, Hamel
Organizational Learning: Argyris, Senge

Index

www.ingramcontent.com/pod-product-compliance
Lightning Source LLC
Chambersburg PA
CBHW071110210326
41519CB00020B/6255